Praise for
The Magic of Newsletter Marketing
The Secret to More Profits and Customers for Life

Who should be sending out newsletters to their customers/clients/patients/prospects? The answer is everybody!!! That's right, there is not a business on the planet that couldn't benefit BIG TIME with a monthly company newsletter. There is no better way to develop a relationship with people than sending out a properly written newsletter and Jim Palmer is the 'go-to' guy to help you get that done. The only criticism I have with Jim's new book is the title. Instead of calling it *"The Magic of Newsletter Marketing,"* I think a more appropriate title would be: *"How to Keep Your Customers Coming Back Again and Again with Newsletters."* Ignoring this book will cause undue risk to your business.

Bill Glazer, President
Glazer-Kennedy Insider's Circle™
www.dankennedy.com

Jim Palmer has put together a true masterpiece for those serious about their business. There is no more powerful way to build your business and consistently nurture your relationship with your customers than this. *The Magic of Newsletter Marketing* is a step-by-step blueprint to growing your business by leaps and bounds . . . no matter what is happening in the economy. This gives you everything you need to master the art and science of ironclad client relationships.

—Troy White
www.CashFlowCalendars.com

Jim has finally drilled down to the core of what most business owners don't understand: a high-value newsletter, as Jim explains it, is the glue that keeps your customers bonded to you for life. This book is not only timely to the changes now happening in our new economy, but it's a MUST-read for any entrepreneur who wants to create customers who stick for life!

—Ari Galper,
Creator of ChatWise www.Chatwise.com
and Unlock The Game www.UnlockTheGame.com

I didn't believe it either. But adding a hard copy newsletter to my business was the best thing I ever did. It increased my credibility, visibility, and profitability virtually overnight. If you don't have a newsletter, you're making a huge mistake by missing the opportunity to develop a deeper relationship with your prospects and clients for maximum profitability. *The Magic of Newsletter Marketing* is THE resource to start with. Jim is the undisputed Newsletter Guru, and his book lays out everything you need to know to start building your own newsletter TODAY. Don't miss out on what I call the biggest secret to building your business that you have probably never considered.

—Nick Nanton, Esq.,
The Celebrity Lawyer & Best-Selling Author
www.CelebrityBrandingYou.com

Jim's book is an incredible resource guide to producing a successful customer newsletter. The single most important way I grew my business in 2008 (yes, even in a recession) was through my newsletter. Jim's book gave me practical ideas that will help me get even more clients. Whether or not you've ever done a newsletter before, the secrets in this book are worth their weight in gold. *The Magic of Newsletter Marketing* is a must-have for every successful entrepreneur.

—Shannon M. McCaffery,
Chief Marketing Implementer
www.marketingimplementer.com

Jim presents you with a proven strategy that makes sense and is simple to use. Newsletters are one of the smartest marketing strategies any business can use, and Jim clearly and easily tells you everything you need to know!

—Susan Berkley,
Owner, The Great Voice Company
www.greatvoice.com

Jim Palmer presents you with a proven and easily doable customer-contact strategy that makes sense and is simple to use. As an internet marketer and Web site conversion strategist, all too often I see marketers and business owners who fail to pick the "low-hanging fruit" of consistent marketing and follow-up, which is a regular customer newsletter. Newsletters are one of the smartest marketing strategies any business can use, and Jim clearly and easily tells you everything you need to know! An absolute MUST-read!

—Adam Hommey,

The Website Surgeon™
www.thewebsitesurgeon.com

Jim Palmer is one of the most brilliant marketing minds I've had the pleasure of doing business with. He truly understands "Relationship Marketing" and details how to build a fence around your prized clients so they come back time after time <u>WITH</u> their friends! I am a BIG fan of Jim's and you will be too after reading this book!

—Eric Paul,
The "High Impact" Marketing and Presentation Expert

I wish a book like this was available when I was learning how to publish newsletters. Today I publish three monthly newsletters, and there were a lot of great tips in this book for me. As a beginner, this book would have made creating newsletters a lot easier. I recommend this book to any business owner who's looking for a reliable marketing tool to generate new customers every month for your business.

—Robert Skrob,
CPA, President, Information Marketing Association
www.Info-Marketing.org

Jim presents you with time-tested, proven strategies that make sense and are simple to use. Newsletters are one of the smartest marketing strategies any business can use, and in *The Magic of Newsletter Marketing*, Jim clearly and easily tells you everything you need to know in his step-by-step formula! He has truly left no leaf unturned. We highly recommend this book to every business person—simple as that—because no matter what business you're in, you should be sending a client newsletter every month.

—Diane Conklin & Gail Saseen,
Complete Marketing Systems, LLC
www.completemarketingsystems.com

Jim's book is for important people to use as a reference and a guide to producing a successful customer newsletter. It's filled with practical ideas that will help you get your newsletter out the door and into your customer's hands!

—Jim Gillespie,
America's Premier Commercial Real Estate Coach℠
www.RealEstateSalesCoach.com

In today's economic reality, smart business owners know strong customer relationships are critical. Jim Palmer knows this, and his book should be required reading for anybody who wants their business to thrive. Do not dismiss this book as something only "newbies" should read. Jim offers wisdom and specific strategies for anybody who calls themselves an entrepreneur.

—Mike Capuzzi,
Inventor, CopyDoodles™
www.CopyDoodles.com

This book has the three essentials for any successful business person: It's easy and quick to read, it's easy to implement and use, and it has a super high return on investment in the book and on your time. Jim Palmer knows how vital a newsletter is for any business, and now you can have customers that stay with you for the price of this book.

—Dave Frees
www.successtechnologies.com

The Magic of Newsletter Marketing is a must-have resource for every entrepreneur and business person. Jim has crafted a step-by-step guidebook that is loaded with expert advice to grow your business. No other marketing tool can demonstrate expertise, establish credibility, and engender loyalty. Better yet, by investing in this resource you bring Jim to the office with you!

—Angela Pipersburgh,
Christian Chamber of Commerce,
Shaddai Marketing and Communications

This easy-to-read book is packed with practical, useful information to help you leverage the power of newsletter marketing to grow your business and gain customers for life. It's a must-read for entrepreneurs.

—Christine Kloser,
Author, *The Freedom Formula*
www.TheFreedomFormula.com

If you're looking for more profits and customers for life—even during a tough economy—then read *The Magic of Newsletter Marketing*. Jim's insight and willingness to share his knowledge are a breath of fresh air in the marketing community.

—Bobby Deraco,
President, Synapse Print Management
www.synapseprint.com

The Magic of Newsletter Marketing is a gem of a book. It has taken our newsletter marketing efforts to a whole new level and the best part is- we're getting great results! Jim Palmer not only tells you how to create a powerful newsletter, he gives you the "whys" as well. This book should be a part of every business resource library!

—Angela V. Megasko, President
Market Viewpoint, LLC
www.marketviewpoint.com

Do you know a friend, colleague, or perhaps a group
that would enjoy and benefit from this book?
If so, I'm happy to extend the following volume discounts!

The Magic of Newsletter Marketing
The Secret to More Profits and Customers for Life

$19.95 U.S.

Special Quantity Discounts
5-20 Books - $16.95
21-50 Books - $13.95
51-100 Books - $11.95
101-250 Books - $8.95
251-500 Books - $6.95

Call or e-mail today to order bulk quantities
800 214 6158
guru@TheNewsletterGuru.com

The Magic of

Newsletter Marketing

The Secret to More Profits and Customers for Life

By Jim Palmer

The Newsletter Guru

With a Foreword by Rob Berkley and Debbie Phillips

CUSTOM NEWSLETTERS, INC.

The Magic of Newsletter Marketing
The Secret to More Profits and Customers for Life
Published by Success Advantage Publishing.
64 East Uwchlan Avenue
Box 231
Exton, PA 19341

ISBN: 978-0615910468

Cover design by Jim Saurbaugh, JS Graphic Design

This book is dedicated to my family,
Stephanie, Nick, Steve, Jessica, and Amanda

Contents

Foreword

For nine months of the year we live and work on Martha's Vineyard. As you can imagine, living and working on an island, no matter how beautiful, peaceful, and inspiring, has its challenges. The population is small, local sources of clients are few, and services can be limited. For anyone to visit takes a concerted and focused effort on his or her part. Plainly, we are off the beaten path.

That said, each year our clients travel from around the world to our island to work with us on Vision Day®—personal, strategic planning days for their work and lives, relationships, and businesses.

We also coach the owners and leaders of public and private companies. Each of us has been doing this work for, well, more than ten years.

The relationships we have with our clients are paramount and extremely important to us. Ours is a very personal business. Our clients are sophisticated, educated, and very resistant to pressure, anything "salesy," or anything inauthentic.

One of the key pillars of our business marketing is our monthly publication of a simple, one-page, two-sided newsletter.

In fact, we have found it to be the single, most effective tool in helping us build and sustain our business. The Vision Day newsletter allows us to communicate with our community in an authentic, clear, and non-promotional voice. From our many readers' enthusiastic responses, we know they read the newsletter, are inspired to work with us, and then remain a part of our community, often referring others.

When we first started publishing our newsletter, we were surprised when people—including former clients whom we hadn't heard from in months or years—called to work with us. Today, we're no longer surprised. Our newsletter recipients frequently tell us that they had been reading our newsletter all along and something in it inspired them to move forward. This is more the rule than the exception.

Our newsletter allows us to keep our community close, and gives us a forum to highlight our clients' successes. Among many other positives, our newsletter helps them understand our points of view about life and work.

Best of all, our newsletter is both fun and easy to write, and we love getting the feedback that people enjoy reading it and find the information useful.

Our success with our Vision Day newsletter is one of the reasons why we were so excited and honored to write the foreword to this book.

Jim Palmer's book, *The Magic of Newsletter Marketing: The Secret to More Profits and Customers for Life*, is the first one to reveal the philosophy, strategies, and tactics for effectively marketing with newsletters to build your business.

In it, he shows you clearly both why and how to use newsletters to retain clients, get new clients, and boost client loyalty. Whatever business or industry you are in, this book will help you produce a newsletter that you can be proud of and use to build your business. Even if you don't think you can write one, his strategies will help you create and publish a newsletter that will inspire your customers and clients.

Jim is a living genius in the business of newsletter marketing, and he can teach you how to get and keep more customers and significantly increase your profits.

When it comes to newsletters, Jim is truly the "Newsletter Guru" and has been a great coach, friend, and mentor to us. In fact, he was pivotal in helping us to launch our Vision Day newsletter, and his organization continues to help us produce it every month.

After nearly two years of monthly Vision Day newsletters, we can attribute a return of 600 percent on our investment! No other form of marketing we do even comes close to the effectiveness of our Vision Day newsletter.

We urge you to take out your highlighter and, with pen in hand, use this book to map out your own successful newsletter strategy. There is no better way to get the true "Newsletter Guru" to sit by your side and help you create a newsletter that will help your business grow by leaps and bounds.

—Rob Berkley and Debbie Phillips

Rob Berkley and Debbie Phillips are pioneers in the field of executive and life coaching, as well as noted authors and speakers. They created and developed Vision Day®, the one-day, strategic planning day for your life. Debbie is the founder of Women On Fire™, an organization dedicated to helping women live their dreams through inspiration, strategies, and support. Vision Day and Rob are featured in the book Speaking of Success, *with Stephen Covey and Brian Tracy. Debbie also is the author of* Women on Fire: 20 Inspiring Women Share Their Life Secrets (and Save You Years of Struggle!)

Rob and Debbie live and work on Martha's Vineyard, Massachusetts, and in Naples, Florida. You can visit them at www.visionday.com or on Facebook.

Foreword

Acknowledgements

A Personal Thank You . . .

Like starting and running a business, writing a book takes considerably more time and effort than first planned on. But also like running a successful business, the end result is very rewarding—it is a real feeling of accomplishment, even before the first book is printed!

First and foremost I want to thank God. His love, patience, wisdom, and the grace He shows me every day is a true blessing. I want to thank my wife, Stephanie, for being my best friend and supporting my dream of owning my own business. She has heard me say more than once, "Next year will be better!" To my children, Nick, Steve, Jessica, and Amanda, thank you for bringing incredible love, joy, and purpose to my life. No matter what else I achieve, nothing will ever mean more to me than my family.

(L-R): Steve, Stephanie, Amanda, Nick, Jessica, and me as we gathered in June 2008 to celebrate my 50th birthday.

I want to thank my parents, Jim and Barbara Palmer, and my in-laws, Cynthia and Anatole Bredikin, for being great role models of what a happy, committed, long-term relationship looks like. Both couples have been married more than fifty years, and that is just too rare these days—way to go! I also want to thank my dad for showing me that you can achieve success in business while also balancing a large family. I have enjoyed and learned from our many conversations about life and business.

I have been blessed with many great friends and mentors. I hesitate to mention names for fear that leaving someone out will be seen as a slight. However, I must mention a few friends who have been instrumental in the growth and success of my business.

I thank Mike Capuzzi for his friendship and never-ending and remarkably insightful marketing and business advice. Mike introduced me to Dan Kennedy and Bill Glazer and played an instrumental role in reshaping my "corporate business" mindset into that of a fast thinking, action-oriented entrepreneur. The countless hours Mike and I spend together masterminding each other's businesses are both a source of inspiration and a great joy.

I met Bobby Deraco in 2004 when he became the print sales rep for my first business, Dynamic Communication. He took meticulous care of my account and we became good friends and subsequent business partners. Bobby introduced me to a revolutionary new print system and then spent nine months working closely with me to develop what would become my second business, No Hassle Newsletters. Bobby's energy, integrity, and unbelievably savvy entrepreneurial vision are a constant source of inspiration to me.

The amazing growth of my business would not be possible without my incredible support team. Thank you to my remarkable personal assistant and client service manager, Kate; my Sensei of my web presence, Adam; my lead designer, Chris; my interview scheduler and head of Pinterest marketing, Jessica; amazing client support team members, Melanie and Lyndsay for providing outstanding client support to our hundreds of valued clients; Amy for her hundreds of 'Newsletter Guru' graphics; Julie-Ann, Sheridan and Matt for leading my team of content writers; Mike and his team from Mikel Mailings for printing and mailing my monthly No Hassle membership programs; Bobby, Jacki, and the entire team at Synapse for being outstanding partners in my Concierge Print and Mail On Demand program; and a special thank you to Tammy Barley for doing a magnificent job editing this book.

I also want to thank Dan Kennedy and Bill Glazer for being amazing mentors. Their newsletters, CDs, DVDs, books, and the value-packed seminars have given me more of an education in a few short years than perhaps my last thirty years in business!

Last but certainly not least, I want to thank the thousands of clients and subscribers whom we have the great pleasure of serving with our Smart Marketing and Business Building Programs, No Hassle Newsletters, No Hassle Social Media, Concierge Print and Mail on Demand, Success Advantage Publishing, No Hassle Infographics, Customer Article Generator, my books, mastermind groups, newsletters, videos, podcasts, and my private coaching program. I can't remember when I've had more fun!

To Your Success,

Jim Palmer

Acknowledgements

Chapter One:
Why Newsletters Are Great
Marketing Tools

Marketing Today Is Tougher Than Ever

How many marketing messages bombard you every day? In 2007 the research firm Yankelovich, Inc. set out to answer that question for people who live in New York City. The answer was five thousand messages a day. Every day. That's the way the world is today—you have to compete for attention.

It's getting harder and harder to stand out from the crowd and get your message through to your customers and prospects. The same Yankelovich study tells us that thirty years ago the number of messages was only two thousand per day.

Ads are everywhere. They're not just in newspapers, on billboards, and on radio and television. You can find ads on video screens, in elevators, and in the back of taxicabs. CBS has even put ads for its shows on supermarket eggs. It seems that if there's a free space anywhere in your life, there will be an ad on it soon.

There are more marketing channels too. There are ads on the Internet, of course, and e-mail messages that fill your inbox with marketing. There's affiliate marketing and viral marketing. And it all means more competition for the scarce attention of your customers and prospects.

That's the bad news. The good news is that newsletters are a simple and cost-effective way to cut through the clutter and tell the people you want to reach all about you.

The Magic of a Customer Newsletter

Newsletters are not perceived in the same manner as a postcard, a flyer or other forms of direct mail marketing. When people receive these or anything else that has a sales and marketing feel to it, their guard goes up and they think, "Uh-oh. What are they trying to sell me?"

Newsletters tend to be informational, making them more welcomed when they are received. As such they have higher readership than other forms of advertising. People also tend to be more receptive to what you have to say in your newsletter because newsletters aren't meant to be sales tools. Rather, they are designed to be a resource.

In one of his No B.S. Marketing Letters, Dan Kennedy put it this way, "People are conditioned to be less resistant to reading information, such as articles, than they are advertising." Since people are conditioned to be less resistant to reading information, which is exactly what a newsletter should be, most people read a newsletter with their guards down.

A customer newsletter is the strongest marketing and business building tool available—bar none.

Newsletters open doors.

That is the magic of why newsletters are such an effective marketing tool—people don't realize they're actually reading something that's going to cause them to buy . . . *if* the newsletter is done correctly. That's the big caveat here. And that's what this book will help you to do. It's the wand that will open doors and bring you customers.

How I Got Started in the Newsletter Business

I discovered the amazing marketing power of newsletters when I ran a bicycle store in the early 1980s. As store manager, a percentage of my income was based on a simple profit system. When the store made more money, I made more money.

I quickly figured out that selling a higher quantity of bicycles was not the best answer to increased earnings. Bicycles generally have a low profit margin and take time to sell, assemble, and service. We needed to concentrate on selling something else, something with a high profit margin. So I did some research.

What I discovered was that of all the items sold in the store, the specialty bicycle clothing had the highest profit margin. I'm specifically talking about the helmets and the fancy jerseys, shorts, gloves, and shoes. The only problem was the lack of demand. In the early '80s a casual bicycle rider did not necessarily want to be

Yes, I am wearing (short) cut off jean shorts and tube socks!

seen in the colorful jerseys and skintight black shorts that are commonplace today. In those days many cyclists simply wore regular shorts.

To prove my case, and at the risk of some embarrassment, I present to you a picture of me heading off to work *before* discovering the advantages of special cycling clothing (left).

This is me cycling with my son, Nick, in beautiful Lancaster County, PA. My father-in-law, Andy Bredikin, is on the left using my bike pump to fix a flat tire.

I rode my bike a lot, and on weekends I rode with my son, Nick, in his bicycle trailer. By the time the second photo was taken (right) I had—thankfully—learned the benefits of wearing the padded gloves, padded shorts, hard-soled shoes, and so on. This clothing made cycling much more enjoyable.

As an avid fan of cycling, and with real world practical experience, I found that when I explained the advantages of bicycle clothing to customers in the store, they too quickly saw the benefits and purchased the bicycle-specific clothing.

Seeing how well we sold clothing face to face, I knew that if I could simply tell (educate) a lot of people about the advantages of bicycle clothing, we would sell much more, which would increase the store's profits, and ultimately my paycheck.

The best way I thought of to communicate with a large audience at one time was to write a newsletter and send it to our entire list of customers.

I typed it out—yes, on an electric typewriter! I explained the advantages of the special clothing, using descriptive language that clearly painted a picture of benefits to the customer. For example, instead of simply writing a headline such as *Monthly Special: Bicycle Shorts*, I wrote a headline that said *The Secret to Riding Four Hours Instead of Forty Minutes Without a Sore Butt!*

I wrote the newsletter in a conversational tone, just the way I would talk to a customer in the store, and I mailed the newsletter to every name we had on the store's customer list. I also used the

---

Newsletter Guru Nugget: Mail your newsletter to everyone in your database. Do not waste time trying to decide who "deserves" your newsletter based on how much they spend or when they last made a purchase. If you have their name and address, send them your newsletter!

newsletter as a prospecting tool and distributed it to the members of the various bicycle clubs within an hour's drive of our store.

Did it work? You bet! Before I started sending the newsletter, our annual sales of clothing were about $8,000 to $10,000. A few years later, we sold $100,000 worth of clothing! In just a few short years I was sold on using newsletters as an effective marketing tool.

But wait, the story gets better.

Several years later, I advanced in my career and became Director of Operations for a national bicycle store franchise called Bike Line. As part of my job, I handled much of this company's marketing efforts, including producing their monthly newsletter.

A typical Bike Line store.

When a prospective franchisee contacted our company from a lead generation ad, in addition to sending them the typical franchise information packet, I also had their names added to the company's mailing list. I remember one prospective franchisee who inquired about a franchise and was initially very excited about opening a store, but then seemed to lose interest. Over several months there was little contact between the prospect and our company. However, since he was on our mailing list, he continued to receive our monthly company newsletter.

Then, nearly eleven months after seemingly losing interest, he recontacted our company and said he was ready to move forward and open his own franchise. That's right, he ultimately decided to purchase a franchise—which was about a $150,000 investment plus royalties!

When our new franchisee came to corporate headquarters to begin his two-week training program, I met with him on the first morning and asked about his initial hesitation to invest with our company. He told me that while he was originally very interested and excited about our company and the prospect of opening his own business, he wasn't 100 percent convinced of our company's stability. That seemed like a fair statement, so I asked him what eventually changed his mind. His answer? While he was reading our newsletter every month, he was learning about our company's continuous growth, reading about various franchise success stories, and how some franchisees were opening their second and third locations. It was after several months of reading about our continued growth and success in our newsletter that he ultimately made the decision to invest in our company.

That is a story with a very happy ending. The end result was a large initial investment plus an ongoing revenue stream for at least ten years.

Newsletter Guru Nugget: Whether you sell a $20 pair of bike shorts or a $150,000 franchise, a monthly newsletter is an amazing marketing tool that can significantly contribute to your growth and profits.

My belief in newsletters as an amazing—almost magical—marketing tool is so strong that in 2001 when I decided to go into business for myself, I knew that newsletters would be my main product offering. And what a ride it's been!

Before we get down to the details of creating a great profit-building newsletter, I want to explain an important marketing concept.

Build a Fence around Your Customers

You want all of your customers to remain close to you. You want the relationship you have with your customers to grow, and you obviously want more repeat business. In addition, every business owner wants their current customers to refer other customers to them.

Being in regular and frequent contact with your customers is known as "Building Your Fence." Your fence is designed to keep your clients and customers *in* and the poachers *out*. A poacher is anyone who is trying to steal your customers. It could be a direct competitor, but it could also be another company that is targeting the same dollars that your customer uses to buy your product or service.

To remain strong and effective, a fence must be properly maintained. If you are not in regular and frequent contact with your customers and clients, your fence will begin to deteriorate, losing one slat or whole sections at a time. Either way, the result is the same. As your fence

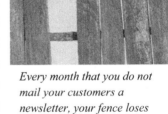

Every month that you do not mail your customers a newsletter, your fence loses another slat.

becomes weaker, you will lose customers and profits.

Let's be practical for a moment. You have probably invested a great deal of time and money growing your business and building your customer list.

If you are not in regular and frequent contact with your customers your fence will deteriorate and eventually be useless.

Don't let your hard work, and the hard-won relationships you have with your customers—and the profits they bring you—slip away by being lazy and not communicating with them.

One of my mentors, marketing genius Dan Kennedy, actually coined the phrase "fence building." One of the best pieces of marketing advice comes from Kennedy's book, *No B.S. Direct Marketing*. "My single biggest recommendation is the use of a monthly customer newsletter. Nothing, and I mean nothing, maintains your fence better."

Commit right now to starting (or restarting) your monthly newsletter. Dollar for dollar, newsletters are the most effective marketing tool available. Plus, customers who read your newsletter are usually in a good position to do business with you again and recommend your product or service to others.

Every time you mail your monthly newsletter you make your fence stronger. Think of this as adding another slat.

No B.S. Direct Marketing

Before we continue, let me just say that in addition to listening to what I have to say in these pages, I strongly encourage you to pick up and read Kennedy's book, *No B. S. Direct Marketing*. I am a voracious reader, and many books have helped me grow my business. But when I

speak, I almost always give credit to this book (I also give away a copy to someone in the audience) as being *the* book that opened my eyes to a different way of marketing and growing a business. If you do not have this book in your library, get it. Once you've read it, you'll kick yourself for not getting it sooner!

Marketing legend Dan Kennedy and The Newsletter Guru.

It was a great pleasure to meet Dan Kennedy at the 2008 Glazer-Kennedy Insiders Circle Super Conference in Nashville, Tennessee where my company was exhibiting as one of Glazer-Kennedy's preferred vendors.

Why Newsletters Are Great Marketing Tools

Chapter Two:
Seven Secret Benefits of
Producing a Newsletter

So far you've seen that newsletters are proven marketing tools that help you to build an all-important fence around your customers or clients. But how exactly does producing a newsletter benefit you and your business?

Here are the seven secret ways newsletters bring sweet success.

Secret # 1: Newsletters Help Keep Customers

No matter what business you are in, your current customers hold the best prospect for future growth. According to research from Bain and Company, getting business from your current customers costs about a fifth of what it costs to acquire a new customer. Not only that, the longer they are customers, the larger their average order is likely to be and the more products or services they're likely to buy.

The 80/20 Rule of Marketing

The 80/20 Rule of Marketing says that 80 percent of a company's profits come from 20 percent of its customers. However, this is backwards from what most companies, especially small businesses, do. Most businesses spend the majority of their marketing time and resources trying to acquire *new* customers. That makes no sense. It is so much easier and quicker to sell to your current customers.

So the right thing to do is to spend 80 percent of your marketing dollars continuing to grow and nurture these existing relationships.

If you'd like to see a short video of me presenting Jim Palmer's 80/20 Rule of Marketing, *please go to* www.NewsletterGuru.tv

You already have an established relationship with your current customers, and they have already purchased from you. This means they find value in what you're selling and they trust you. This is a huge hurdle that we all have to overcome when we are prospecting for new customers—a hurdle that you've already overcome with your current customers.

A regular newsletter helps you stay top-of-mind with your current customers. Your newsletter arrives and instantly your customers are thinking about you. After receiving your newsletter on a consistent basis, your customers actually begin to look forward to receiving it—it's a welcomed friend—and they are curious to see what tips you are sharing with them this issue.

Issue after issue, your newsletter reinforces your relationship with your customers. It makes your fence stronger. It also gives you a way to tell current customers about products and services you provide that they may not know about.

Secret # 2: Newsletters Help Get New Customers

You want your newsletter to help you get more new customers. Good, informative articles give your newsletter what marketing pros call "pass-along value." Since your customers value your products or services, they'd like to tell other people about them, but most of them just don't know how. Your newsletter makes it easy.

When a customer passes along one of your newsletters to a friend or colleague, two wonderful things happen. First, you get a referral. Referrals are great for you because people believe and trust their friends and business colleagues more than they believe any marketing message. The second wonderful thing is that customer doesn't just hand over the newsletter. He or she usually points to a specific article or information item and says, "You should look at this. I do business with these people." Now your newsletter is in the hands of a prospect, and it's more than a marketing piece. It's been customized by the referral to tell your prospect about a specific product or service.

No wonder a friendly pass-along is one of the best ways your newsletter can help you get new customers. But it's not the only one.

Because people read newsletters as a publication and not a marketing piece, a newsletter is a great way to tell potential customers about your business in all kinds of situations. Here are some ideas:

- Mail your newsletter to all current and past customers, as well as to any prospects that have requested information about your company. Include any other marketing materials that may hook their interest.
- Your salespeople should hand out copies of your newsletter when they make sales calls. Integrate the newsletter into the sales process. Point out special articles or news items that your customer will be interested in.
- Place a stack of newsletters at businesses frequented by customers. This can turn into a simple cross-promotion. One golf coach I know places her newsletter in a chiropractor's waiting room and hands out the

chiropractor's newsletter as part of an information packet she gives her clients.

- Put a stack on the information table at community events.
- Place copies in the information rack at the Chamber of Commerce.
- Give out your newsletters at trade shows and exhibition booths.
- Post a PDF copy of your newsletter on your company's Web site.
- Put them in the envelopes with your checks when you pay bills.

Secret # 3: Newsletters Help Build Credibility

Newsletters help you build credibility because when people read your brochure, they treat it as a piece of marketing literature. But when those same people read your newsletter, they read it like a publication.

Your newsletter also gives you the opportunity to tell people stories about what you do and how well your products work. You can illustrate the benefits of your product or service with statistics and with customer testimonials.

Secret # 4: Newsletters Help You Stand Out from Your Competition

Because you are deciding the direction and content of each newsletter, you are differentiating yourself from others—especially the larger businesses who typically do not produce customer newsletters.

Secret # 5: Newsletters Are an Excellent Way to Enhance Your Reputation as an Expert in Your Industry

This is extremely important for this reason: Your customers may not be ready or need your product or service today, but when they are, they want an experienced professional. And through your newsletter, you've been able to build a relationship and the reputation of an expert. People want to do business with someone they trust, so when they are ready for what you offer, they'll turn to you.

Secret # 6: Newsletters Help You Build Your Brand

Branding is the art of making people aware of who you are, what you do, and how you're different from and better than the competition.

Many marketing authorities cover the subject of branding with a lot of mumbo jumbo. Here are the basics, plain and easy: You want to have a little bell go off in people's heads when they hear your name. You want them to say to themselves, "Oh yes, they're the people who . . ."

Establishing this brand recognition is pretty much a numbers game. How many numbers depends on which expert you choose to listen to.

Marketing expert Dr. Jeffrey Lant says you should contact people seven times in eighteen months to make your brand stick. In their book *Marketing Boot Camp*, Arnold Sanow and Dan McComas put the number at nine times in eighteen months. Other marketing research suggests that once a month is a good frequency.

I've been doing customer newsletters for almost thirty years. I've read the research, and I've seen the results clients get with different mailing frequencies. My research and experience tell me that to get the best results from a newsletter you need to send it out, like clockwork, every month.

If a decision maker gets your newsletter every month, he or she will remember you and what you do. That's because of the ways newsletters are different from other marketing materials. (What comes on an infrequent basis? Junk mail.)

Think about some of the magazines you receive—*Time, Redbook, Readers Digest,* or some other publication. These magazines are delivered to your home on the same two to three days each month. This helps cement a higher value to the magazine, and it becomes a welcomed guest and not an annoying pest.

The same can be said about your newsletter. When it is delivered at the same time each month, it will build up that same level of importance. It will help build your brand.

Secret # 7: Newsletters Have a Longer Shelf Life than Other Types of Marketing

Think about this. Newsletters can be taken anywhere. They are received at the office, but are taken home, on a plane, to the kids' soccer games—everywhere. And when the newsletters are informative, fun, and easy to read, they are not thrown away. They are kept and referenced. Plus, newsletters are often read by multiple readers. People pass along newsletters to friends, business associates, or even their neighbor. This is a *huge* benefit of producing a newsletter.

Don't Just Take My Word for It

You don't have to take my word for all of this. You can listen to what other experts have to say about the benefits of newsletter marketing.

As mentioned previously, Dan Kennedy is one of the most widely respected marketing experts in the world. I mentioned this earlier but it warrants repeating. In his book *No B.S. Direct Marketing*, Kennedy said, "My single biggest recommendation is the use of a monthly customer newsletter."

"Well," you might be saying, "he may be an expert, but that's just his opinion." Okay then, here's a quote from Bank Marketing. You know how conservative bankers can be.

"Statistically validated and reliable surveys show that 75 percent of readers remember seeing an issue of their bank's newsletter, and over 50 percent of them read every or almost every issue. Better yet, newsletters generate response and cross-selling opportunity—a full 24 percent of readers said newsletter articles led them to request more information, respond to an offer, or do more business with the publishing bank."

You still might be skeptical. You might think that a strategy that sounds so simple won't get results for someone like you. Fortunately, I've been helping clients use newsletters to improve their profit for almost three decades. That means I've got lots of clients and I can let them speak for themselves.

How about this from mortgage banker Ken Pitts? "Every time we mail our mortgage newsletter, *The Home Connection*, we get at least one new client by way of referral!"

Or how about this from marketing manager Rebecca Monroe? "Our President/CEO and VP of Sales/Marketing believe that the newsletter is one of our best marketing tools."

I'll share one last testimonial before we move on. Austin B. Meadows, president and CEO of Security Cubed, shared this with me about his newsletter: "I am in front of my customers every month. Many call me to say how much they enjoy the newsletter and thank me for sending them. I even have customers call me with their changes of address so they don't miss an issue! Most important, my referral rate has increased significantly."

If you still want more, there are lots of testimonials on my Web site, www.NoHassleNewsletters.com.

Now that you know just how a newsletter can benefit you, it's time to show you how to generate a magical, profit-producing newsletter.

Chapter Three: Planning Your Newsletter Effort

It doesn't take any more work to produce a great newsletter than a run-of-the-mill newsletter. You've still got to pull the material together, create the content, and format it. It takes the same effort to send it.

Knowing that, why not spend the same amount of effort and resources and make your newsletter great? There are lots of ways to do a bad newsletter, but great newsletters all begin the same way—with a plan that evolves from a few simple questions.

Questions to Ask Yourself

Before you start producing newsletters, you need to stop and think about what you want to achieve. A great newsletter isn't just about the newsletter itself. It's also about the customer's needs and the way the newsletter works with your other marketing efforts.

Following are questions I often cover in the first conversations I have with clients for custom newsletters. At the end of this chapter you will find a Newsletter Planning Program Form with these same questions summed up to help you organize your thoughts.

→ **Who will read the newsletter?**

Here's the cold hard truth about your customer newsletter. It's not about you and what you want to write about. It's about what your customers want to read and what is of interest to them.

You've heard that you must "know your audience." A good way to do that is to get a mental image of your target customer when writing and designing your newsletter. Here's how. Think about who your average customer is. It could be male or female. It could be a certain age. It could be a certain demographic. Try and get a detailed picture of the unique qualities of your target customer.

Next, go online and find a picture of what you imagine this person looks like, then put that picture on your desk. As you're writing, just keep looking at that picture and write as if you're having a conversation with that person. It sounds a little hokey, but it's a very cool exercise, one that brings impressive results.

Visualizing your customer becomes very easy if you think of a specific person you can use as a reference point. You already have customers and you want to meet their needs. If your customer is Art Jones, and you're going to send the newsletter to Art, use him as your mental picture.

Newsletter Guru Nugget: Concentrate on your perfect target customer when writing your newsletter.

You'll get much more insight if you ask, "What would Art like?" than you will if you ask, "What will my customers like?" You'll have a better idea of what to write about if you ask, "What questions has Art asked me?" Instead of "What questions do my customers ask?"

Then when you prepare and write your newsletter, close your eyes, picture "Art," and write to that person. Imagine yourself having a conversation with him, and the conversation becomes newsletter articles. Your goal is to make sure that Art stays engaged in the conversation and thanks you when you're done. If you do that, you'll connect with a huge amount of people on your list.

→ What problems do my customers have? What do they want to know about?

Great customer newsletters are filled with things that customers want to read. Most customers want to read articles and stories that are interesting and informative. Sure, some articles will obviously have to do with your company, products, and services. But there is a limit to how much your newsletter should be about your company, or you risk turning it into another sales/marketing piece—and that's not the goal of a newsletter. If customers perceive your newsletter as just another marketing piece, they will not eagerly read it every month.

I recommend you maintain a 50/50 ratio—50 percent of your newsletter focused on your business, products, and services (I call this "work stuff") and the other 50 percent on the "other stuff." The other stuff consists of articles and stories that are fun, interesting, and informative, and typically have nothing to do with your business.

I'll give you a big clue—while the other stuff has nothing to do with your company, it is the real secret to the success of many customer newsletters. It is what your customers enjoy reading, and as such, they keep reading your newsletter. That builds top-of-mind awareness for you and your company.

You may be asking, "Jim, what do you mean by the 'other stuff'?" I am talking about short, interesting, and informative articles, factoids, tips, cartoons, humor, and sometimes even puzzles. The secret is, this is what your customers enjoy reading, no matter what business you're in. This is what they look forward to, what brings a smile to their faces.

Reader's Digest is one of the most widely subscribed to magazines. It is largely a collection of stories on a variety of subjects, and one of their most popular categories is humor. This should not come as much of a shock when you consider that so much of what we read and hear is either bad news or negative. People appreciate reading good news. They appreciate learning something, and they particularly appreciate when you *do not bore them*.

Newsletter Guru Nugget: The kiss of death for any newsletter is being boring.

If your newsletter informs, educates, and entertains—with a special emphasis on entertains—they will read it month after month. If you give them a newsletter that focuses too much on your business, products, and services, they will not likely read it every month, and you will come to the conclusion that newsletters are not very effective.

The "other stuff" is so important, and so needed, it is the reason that I created my flagship program, No Hassle Newsletters.

No Hassle Newsletters (www.NoHassleNewsletters.com) is my monthly newsletter content and ready-to-use newsletter template program. To help people create and send their customer newsletters every month, I supply subscribers with twenty-four pages of my Famous Customer-Loving Content ™ (the "other stuff") covering a wide range of topics that they are free to use in their newsletters. I also provide subscribers with ready-to-use newsletter templates to remove the hassle of designing their newsletter. The newsletters are provided in MS Word so that they are quick and easy for anyone to edit. So, if you want to have your monthly newsletter about 90 percent ready to go even before you write a single word, go to www.NoHassleNewsletters.com and join hundreds of other entrepreneurs in nine countries as a successful newsletter marketer.

So what makes good content for the "work stuff" part of your newsletter? Think about the questions your customers ask you. Those answers make great copy for your newsletter.

Let's say you have a chiropractic practice. Patients have heard about carpal tunnel syndrome and ask questions about it. Patients know that chiropractors deal with back pain, so they ask you all kinds of back pain questions when they come in the door. And if you're a chiropractor, you get questions about general health issues like keeping kids healthy.

All of those questions and concerns can be turned into articles for your newsletter. Help your readers solve a problem. Answer their questions.

Conversely, say you are an accountant. Each month you send a newsletter jammed with information—about tax laws or pending legislation that Congress is considering. As this accountant's customer, would you read it? No! That's what you pay your accountant for—to know the tax laws and follow his industry.

Don't make your newsletter about your business. No matter what business you're in, you know your customers' problems. You know the questions they ask. That's what your newsletter should be about.

I actually created my very first newsletter about bicycle clothing with the help of my readers. I connected with my readers on a very personal level because I spent an awful lot of time on the sales floor, and really knew who they were. I knew what their pains were. And that's what I addressed when I was writing.

As I said before, your newsletter is not about what's important to you—it's about what's important to your customers. Every month identify your customer' needs and wants, give them solutions, and yes, even entertain them, and you're on your way to a great newsletter.

But you also need to consider your business objectives.

Action Step: Take out two sheets of paper. On one, make a list of your customers' problems. On the other, make a list of the most frequent questions they ask. Get help from your staff, especially your front line staff. It is likely that this exercise will provide your editorial content for a year or more!

A Business Publication

It's important to keep your newsletter customer-focused, but you must also remember that you're producing a newsletter to help your business do what the father of modern management, Peter Drucker, said was the goal for all businesses: to create and keep customers.

With a newsletter, you want to always remind your customers of how much value you deliver so that they won't even think of considering a competitor. A newsletter is designed to help your business get and keep more customers, and to increase your profits by boosting your repeat and referral business.

Be sure to remember that the ultimate goal of your newsletter is to increase your profits (just like it was my goal when managing the bicycle shop).

You want to get more business from your current customers. If you do a great job for your customers, they will love you for it.

The problem is that they don't know all the ways you can do a great job. You can let them guess. You can let them look somewhere else for the products or services you could provide. Or, you can use your newsletter to tell them about all the ways you can help them.

Work Stuff: Tell Your Customers What Else You Do

The first "work stuff" secret to generating a profit-producing newsletter is to tell your customers what else you do. This is huge! Many customers will engage in business with you and perhaps do repeat business with you over the same few products or services because they are completely unaware of your other offerings.

What problems do my customers have? What do they want to know about?

Take the insurance guy as an example. He may handle a company's business insurance, but his customers may not even be aware that he also handles homeowners and auto insurance. He's probably missing out of many business opportunities simply because his current customers have him pigeonholed as their business insurance guy, not their personal insurance guy too.

Or, as before, let's say you're an accountant. You do your customers' taxes and perhaps their financial statements. They know that. They may not know that you can also help them with business planning. Use your newsletter to share the story of how you've helped another client with business planning. Mention that you can help clients with planning, and invite them to call.

Don't miss out on these opportunities. Use your newsletter to educate your customers on what other products and services you provide.

Work Stuff: Tell Them What's New

The second "work stuff" secret to generating a profit-producing newsletter is to tell your customers what's new. As business owners, we're always coming up with new products or services, and using your newsletter is an excellent vehicle for these announcements. Every time you come up with a new product or service, write about it in your newsletter. Remember to think from the standpoint of **What problems do my customers have? What do they want to know about?**

For this type of article—a product-related article—you obviously want to list the name of the new product as well as the benefits it provides. This could work for services also. Talk about some of the causes or uses, and describe how your new products will benefit them. That's how you're going to connect with people, your target audience. Include some stories of how other people have used them and the success that they've had using your product or service. (I'll discuss writing success stories in Chapter Five.)

→ What other marketing pieces of ours will customers see? How will those pieces work with the newsletter?

Ask yourself these questions when planning your newsletter effort to help you focus on your overall marketing plan. The newsletter won't be the only way your customers will get information about you and what you do. Other possibilities include personal sales calls, telephone sales calls, voice mail, advertisements, postal mail, e-mail, an e-mail newsletter, and your

Newsletter Guru Nugget: Whatever your business, a highly effective newsletter is one that provides a proper balance—where the content is not all about business ("work stuff")!

Web site. What are some other ways you will connect with your customers?

Action Step: Make a list of other ways that your customers and prospects get information about you and what you do.

Once you've got your list of contacts and information sources, spend some time analyzing how your other forms of marketing will work with the newsletter and how the newsletter can make them more effective.

→ What is our newsletter name?

The masthead is the major graphic element at the top of the first page of the newsletter. It includes the newsletter title. The masthead should identify your company. It may say that you "present" the newsletter title. It may include your logo or a symbol that represents your kind of business. A spine is a good symbol for a chiropractor. A professional speaker might be represented by a microphone.

In most cases, the newsletter title you develop should not be the name of the company. It should, however, be a name that sticks in the mind, that rolls pleasantly from the tongue, and, along with your graphic of choice, easily conveys what the newsletter is about.

→ What is our tagline?

The tagline is at the bottom of the masthead. You can think of it as a subtitle. The tagline for *Information Assurance* (you can see the graphic in Chapter Four) is *News and Information Dedicated to the Awareness and Advancement of Information Security.*

The newsletter title and the tagline should work together. They should tell anyone who picks up your newsletter what it's about. It should give them a clue about the benefits of reading the newsletter.

→ How often will we mail our newsletter?

To expand what I touched on in Secret # 6: Newsletters Help You Build Your Brand, here is the most important secret to generating a profit-producing newsletter: **Consistency trumps everything else.** Great newsletters show up like clockwork. You can count on them reaching you every month with solid information, helpful tips, and good ideas. Consistency far outweighs the size of a newsletter, whether it's color or black and white, or even the quality of the content. This may be the most important thing you learn in this book.

You simply must have frequency to build trust and relationships. That trust and those relationships turn into business and a long term competitive edge.

A common mistake that many newsletter writers make is the failure to be consistent. If you aren't consistent with your newsletter, it doesn't matter what content it contains. It becomes junk mail—just another pest—that your customers receive every once in a while.

Consider it in these terms. Magazines and other publications arrive monthly on schedule. Junk mail in all of its various forms arrives sporadically. In what category do you want your newsletter to be perceived?

Newsletter Guru Nugget: Consistency is the most important characteristic of great newsletters. Mail them the same time every month.

I strongly recommend monthly newsletters because when they are produced monthly on a regular schedule, they have a higher perceived value. They build a stronger bond and brand with your customers, and your customers begin to look forward to them. If you publish less often, you lose that important top-of-mind position. If you publish more often, there will be customers who think you're bombarding them with marketing messages.

It's also vital that you publish your newsletter *every* month. That way you develop habits and get into the rhythm of production. You and your contributors will know when copy and pictures should be done, so you'll all be on the lookout for good information and pictures. You'll know when the newsletter will be mailed. Your salespeople will know when the next issue will be available.

That will also set up expectations for your customers. Your customers will get used to hearing from you at the same time every month. They'll look forward to the fun, interesting, and readable content of your newsletter.

You'll find that the regular schedule will aid your other marketing efforts too. If you've got a special sales promotion planned, for example, you can alert people in the newsletter for two months prior. Then, when it's promotion time, your promotional efforts will have the way paved for them by your newsletter articles. Your salespeople can hand out newsletters as promotion flyers.

Newsletter Guru Nugget: Decide to publish your newsletter monthly, and then stick to it! Missing a month (or more) will cause your fence to fall into disrepair.

Send your newsletter every month and you'll build better relationships, improve customer retention, and draw more new customers.

→ What should be in every issue?

The final question to ask yourself when planning your newsletter effort is another point of consistency. What should appear in every issue?

While we discuss the *what*, let's also briefly consider the *where*. Dependability is more than just sending out your newsletter at the same time every month. It's being consistent with the kinds of articles you include and where you place regular articles. Of course, your readers are smart enough to find their favorite article by hunting around, but why make them work for it? Why make extra work for yourself by plotting a whole new layout each month?

One of the most important elements of a great newsletter is what I refer to as "your personal monthly message." This can be as short as a paragraph, but the main idea is to show some of your personality to your customers—break down the "company" façade. Your personal monthly message is where you can make a personal connection by talking about non-transactional things, such as an interesting vacation. The whole idea is to let your customers see you as a person, and not simply a business.

Great newsletters use the same basic layout every time. The most important stories in your newsletter should be in the same place in every issue. Follow the lead of the *Wall Street Journal*. The *Wall Street Journal* has the same basic layout every business day. Readers don't have to wonder where to find the top story. It's always in the same spot.

If you go into your grocery store, you always know you can zoom up this aisle and zoom down here to get the bread. You know exactly where the milk is. Now once in a while your grocery store will move things around because they want to have you look at more items. I'll be honest with you, that ticks me off. So don't do that in your newsletter. Make sure you're consistent with the kinds of articles you include and with the format of where you place them.

With that in mind, we can now plan what should be in every issue. You should have the following: a main article, a back page article, other stories, regular features, an offer, and a response mechanism. We'll discuss each of those next. For your convenience, you will find an Issue Planning Form master at the end of the chapter with these points listed along with a box for the names of the individuals you assign the articles to and a second box for the articles' due dates so you'll have them in time for publication. Copy the form as needed. Use it to help you plan every issue.

Most Important Spaces: The Main Article

The main story of a newsletter is typically found on the front page. The main article is one of the most important stories in your newsletter. As the lead "work stuff" article, this is usually where you will write about your products and services. Take note that when you write about your products and services, it is important to do so in a way that does not appear to be selling your customers anything. Remember, your customers expect to read information, not sales brochures.

One way to achieve this balancing act is to tell other customers' **success stories**. Share how a customer benefited from using one of your products or services and, if possible, include a customer testimonial and evidence of the benefit received.

The main story on the front page is also a good place to tell your customers what else you do. Keep in mind that customers usually begin a relationship with you based on a single transaction. Unless you're the greatest sales person in the world or have the most unbelievable follow-up program, chances are very good that your customers are unaware of the many other products you sell or services you provide.

I want to give you another big secret on why monthly customer newsletters are so effective. It is because you are marketing and communicating with people who are already *buyers*.

Action Step: On a blank sheet of paper, draw a line down the middle. In the left column, make a list of every product or service you offer. In the right column, note a specific customer who's used that product or service. When complete, you will have several months of "main articles" already mapped out!

Put your main article in the same place every time and make it easy for your readers.

Special note: No article, including the main article, should "continue" more than once, or at all, if possible. Don't make your reader constantly flip through the pages to finish reading an article.

Most Important Spaces: The Back Page Article

The back page of your newsletter is not simply the mailing panel. It is the first thing your readers will see when the newsletter comes out of the mailbox or when he or she comes upon the newsletter in a stack of mail. The back page is the second highest valued piece of real estate of your newsletter. Here's why.

The vast majority of newsletters are designed as self-mailers and folded. On one side of the fold is the mailing panel. On the other side is the prime real estate section, because when a newsletter arrives, other than the mailing panel, this is the first section of the newsletter that is seen—and usually read. You want your second most important message to go in this section.

Here's an example of how I used the back panel to increase profits for one of my clients, an HVAC dealer. He wanted to increase his profits by introducing a new product line—whole house generators. We wrote an article addressing the benefits of investing in a whole-house generator, included a picture, and placed it on the back page of his newsletter. This newsletter generated thirteen inquiries, and each generator sells for approximately $6,000. By using the back panel to introduce this new line of products, he not only educated his customers on a new product available to them, but he also increased his revenues.

This is also a great place to make a personal connection with your customers using "personality based" writing (more on personality based writing in Chapter Five) in a personal monthly message. On many of the newsletter templates that I provide at No Hassle Newsletters (www.NoHassleNewsletters.com) I include an article area called "Personal Monthly Message" to help you.

When planning your newsletter effort, determine what kind of back page article will work best for your business this month.

Other Stories

"How in the world do I come up with so much content every month?" you ask? Earlier I suggested including informative articles, factoids, tips, cartoons, humor, and puzzles. Here we'll sum up some of those content ideas and come up with more. You may find it helpful to flag this section as your Other Stories Brainstorming Section.

Customers love to learn new things. You're the expert on your business and what you do. Tell them about new developments. Introduce them to new products or services. Give tips for using existing products or services. Think of new uses for those products or services. Offer them articles that help them learn.

Short, helpful articles about services you offer are the kind of pieces that generate pass-along referrals. Pass-along value makes your newsletter a great way for your current customers to refer you to their friends and colleagues.

If you run a house cleaning service, you know that your customers do some cleaning when you're not there. Your newsletter should share cleaning tips your customers can use. That way your value goes beyond the cleaning you actually do.

The chiropractor can do a short piece on back pain. The accountant can share *Five Things Every Business Plan Should Have.*

Readers love leadership-management tips. They love to read articles on saving money; in winter, for example, you might include the tips section *Five Things You Can Do to Save Money on Your Heating Bill.* Readers find such tips informative, helpful, and enjoyable.

Customers love stories. Don't just describe what you do. There are certain times when you're writing articles in your newsletter where you can be selling. After all, newsletters are sales letters in disguise. But there's a way to do that so that it reads like a success story. Demonstrate your benefits for your customers by telling them a story about someone like them who succeeded because they purchased your product or service. Here's what I mean.

Instead of describing a product or service, paint a story that illustrates the benefits of the product or service. Instead of using the headline *XYZ Insurance Company Announces New Coverage,* say *New Line of Coverage Saves Small Manufacturer $23,000 in Insurance Premiums.* This is a much more effective headline. It grabs the readers' attention. It allows you to share one of your success stories and gets readers thinking, "I wonder if this coverage would work for me?"

What you're doing is providing information. It's all about good information. But you're doing it in a way that's going to cause people to think, "Hmm, I could benefit from that."

This is an extremely effective way to make your newsletter more interesting while still meeting your ultimate goal of generating more profits for your business.

In addition to the stories of how others are using your products and services, include testimonials. One question I get a lot is, "Jim, how do you get testimonials?" If you've seen No Hassle Newsletters, you know I have a lot of testimonials there. Here's my secret to doing that. Ready? *I ask.* That's all I do. I ask people, "Would you be willing to give a testimonial?" The best time to ask is right after I do a job and they're happy with it.

Recently I launched a new joint venture project, and the first issue went out and the customers are very happy. And I said, "Obviously you've seen my Web site. You know I'm a fan of testimonials. I'd love to get one from you." Following my own advice about taking action, I continued, "Write it up and e-mail it to me." I told them exactly what to do and how to do it. That's how I've gained and collected so many testimonials. Your business would benefit from collecting testimonies as well.

What other story ideas do you have? Are there other pieces you can use to provide sidebars or extra information about the main stories? Be creative.

Customers love things that are cheap, or better, free. Mention a special product or service or an upcoming promotion. Or come up with samples or trial offers to get them to return to your business. For example, if you have a coaching program, a lot of folks do a "first, second, and third month is free," and then the client's investment begins after that.

Customers love a little humor. Just because newsletters are serious business doesn't mean you should be long-faced and serious all the time. Lighten your message with gentle humor. Obviously you'll want to use non-offensive humor.

One of the things that I talk about a lot is *Reader's Digest.* *Reader's Digest* is a magazine about not really much of anything.

There are short stories, quips, and so on. Their surveys have shown that the most popular thing people read—and read first—is the humor.

Another thing you can do is welcome new clients. This is a great way to say who you are currently working with. That is using the power of association. Often you see partial lists of customers on a business's Web site or in their brochure, if they do those. (I'm not a fan of brochures.) Those customers' names can draw notice to your business, especially if you have some recognizable names.

I want to share a really quick story with you. When I first got started in the newsletter business, I went down to the local Target store. I knew they did an internal newsletter, and I said to the manager, "Let me redesign your newsletter. I'm going to do it for free. The only thing that I ask is that I can promote on my Web site that I'm doing your newsletter."

What I did from there is I listed Target and the Target logo on my Web site as a client. I did not specify that it was the Target of the town I live in. I just put Target. When I met with other perspective clients, I said, "By the way, I'm doing Target's newsletter," which was true and accurate. It carried weight. Welcoming new customers or clients makes for good content—the new people feel welcome, your current customers become aware of new directions your business is going, and the power of association benefits you.

Try adding client profiles. Client profiles can be great sales tools, though I recommend you keep them short and to the point. A client profile that's a page long is a real yawn, and people will not read that.

When I do client profiles, or when I do them for my corporate clients, I ask clients questions in the form of an interview, questions that I know will elicit the answers that I want. For example, "How has using this product benefited your company?" You can either use their answers verbatim, or you may edit them a little bit, depending on how their answers go. Then you can turn that content into an article.

Use customer quotes. By doing so you are letting your customers sell for you. Customer quotes are like testimonials, but they're just a little different.

A testimony is usually something about you and your company, and/or how your products and services have helped. A customer quote may be only a sentence or two that supports an article you're writing, so it isn't the same as a full-blown testimonial. You can find quotes in letters and e-mails of appreciation from your customers. When I find a good quote—whether it's in print or in an e-mail—I put it in a newsletter, often on a graphic that looks like a yellow legal pad, so that it stands out as a line from a letter written by a satisfied customer.

Answers to customer surveys work well. Sometimes you'll conduct surveys, if you are a brick and mortar or if you're selling a certain product. Sometimes the company of the product you're selling will conduct surveys. You can feature those in your newsletter.

Employee spotlights are another great way to inject pizzazz into your newsletter. I think, in general, the usual way that you see employee spotlights is kind of boring. You know, This is Michelle. She takes care of AR. Michelle's favorite hobbies are horseback riding and whatever. It's just not important news worthy of your customers' time.

But there's a way you can do it and here it is. If you do an employee spotlight, do it in a way that highlights their particular skills, their experience level, or perhaps the impressively large company they used to work for. An employee spotlight written this way makes your customers feel good about doing business with you because you have high quality employees.

If you need more ideas or don't have time every month to think up your own (shameless plug coming), check into subscribing to No Hassle Newsletters. Successful newsletters require good external content. The trouble with most newsletters is that they overkill on such a narrow subject range. Even the most dedicated reader is eventually going to switch off.

Great newsletters should have good 50/50 balance of work stuff and other stuff—they must be informative, enlightening, and entertaining! The other stuff is what I put in No Hassle Newsletters, the things that just about anybody reading a newsletter is going to find fun and enjoyable. I often say that No Hassle Newsletters is the *Reader's Digest* for people who put out newsletters.

It's a fact that people enjoy reading the other stuff more than the work stuff. Sorry to say it, but it's true. One of my large corporate clients is a Chamber of Commerce with about two thousand members. Whenever I go to a meeting people tell me, "Jim, I love the tips you put in there, the management, the leadership. I love the HR tips." And I say, "What about the other articles?" Here's the answer I often get, "Why would I want to read about what the Chamber did last month?"

It may be a little bit different in your business, but I would wager a nice lunch it's not. So take great care what you put in your newsletter to make sure there's a good balance of the work stuff versus the other stuff.

The Consistent Elements of a Great Newsletter

Every newsletter you send out should be filled with interesting, informative, and entertaining articles. The mix of topics will be slightly different every month. However, great newsletters typically contain one or two things that are in every issue. These will be your regular features.

> *Newsletter Guru Nugget:* Decide what feature(s) should be in every issue. Use the Newsletter Program Planning Form to help you organize your thoughts about newsletter strategy.

Your regular features will depend on who you are and what your newsletter is about. For example, a newsletter about fitness will always have fitness tips and perhaps healthy eating tips. A salon newsletter may always have a feature about grooming and nail care, and perhaps a cartoon about the salon business. The exact elements will vary for each newsletter.

The point to remember is that if you begin a relationship with your customers through your monthly newsletter, and they come to enjoy the regular feature, don't disappoint them by not including it one month. A good example of a regular item that thousands of people count on is the cartoon graphic on the front page of *USA Today*. It is always interesting and, more importantly, it is always included in every paper. Regular features help establish your unique identity.

A mortgage lender may want to include a "Mortgage News" segment in every letter. A cleaning company might decide on a "Cleaning Tip of the Month." A professional service firm might want to include at least one client story/testimonial.

An Offer

Don't miss the opportunity to ask your readers to contact you. Give them a reason to do so. You can offer them a special report, a tip sheet, a free consultation, a demonstration of a new product, just about anything that will entice them to contact you.

When you want to include the occasional promotion or discount, be very cautious where you place it since it will be read as an advertisement. I recommend that when you include one, do so as an insert. Do not put it in the body of the newsletter.

Why? One of the reasons newsletters work so well is because they are not perceived as another piece of marketing material, like a postcard or a flier. They are perceived as welcome information and good entertainment.

The minute you start promoting or including coupons in the body of your newsletter, your newsletter becomes perceived as being another marketing piece, and it will lose its effectiveness. People will cautiously open subsequent issues, thinking, "Okay, what are they going to sell me this month?" So be certain your newsletter does not come across as a marketing ploy.

In your wording, try to avoid using vague phrases like "within ten days of receiving this letter," because you don't know when exactly the post office will deliver it or when they're going to read it. Instead, be precise. "This offer expires at 4 p.m. Eastern time on March 6th." There's no question what you mean when you say it like that.

When choosing the color of your promotion page, consider this. Newsletters are often black ink on white paper. Print your special offer on canary paper or light green or light blue. Many people, particularly those not expecting an advertisement, prefer pastel colors to those screaming neon ones.

A Response Mechanism

The offer alone is not enough. Make it easy for them to respond. That can be a coupon or just a phone number. With your call to action, always give clear instructions on how to reply. I suggest that you include more than one way for your customers to respond. For example, if you were running a contest and asked your customers to reply by e-mail, keep in mind that there are some people, believe it or not, who do not have or use e-mail. Giving multiple response options such as e-mail, Web site, fax, or telephone gives you the best chance to for the highest response.

Different Newsletters for Different Customer Groups

I've often been asked, "Is it wise to send the same newsletter to different customer groups?" For instance, perhaps you own a business that has both retail and wholesale customers. My answer: more than likely it's not a good idea, and I'll tell you why, but have no fear. Sending two newsletters is not as difficult as you may think.

If you have two or more different customer groups (here we'll use our example of a business that has both retail and wholesale customers), obviously you're going to write a separate personal monthly message, because if you're talking with wholesale customers you're generally talking a different language. Wholesalers have a different language than retailers. You might use certain jargon or buzzwords. Any special offer, obviously, will need to be tailored two different ways.

And of course, if you're going to do a customer profile, you'll want to write about one of your wholesale customers in the newsletter that goes out to your wholesale customers, and you will profile a retail customer in the newsletter that goes out to your retail customers. If you do otherwise, people will be confused about what you're doing. (Remember, know your customer and gear the newsletter toward him or her.)

Here's how to make this fairly easy on yourself. You don't need to customize each entire newsletter. The only place you really have to customize is the article on the front, which is usually your work stuff, and your article on the back page, which is usually your personal monthly message. Your other content as well as your contact information will probably remain the same.

Planning an Individual Issue

When you send your newsletter every month, you'll get into a rhythm that will make producing your newsletter easier. The Issue Planning Form at the end of this chapter will help you to coordinate your efforts each month and to complete your tasks on time.

The Timeline

This will become routine, but it's still a good idea to write down the key due dates every month and share them with everyone who needs to know. At a minimum you should have target dates for the following:

- Deciding on the main story and back story
- Deciding on other company-focused stories that will go in the newsletter
- Select other non-company-focused articles to provide balance
- When stories need to be completely written and edited
- When pictures should be selected
- When captions will be written
- When you will do the final review before sending the newsletter to production
- When the copy and pictures go out for production
- When the finished newsletters will be available
- When the newsletters will be mailed and distributed

What I like to suggest is that you put a recurring appointment in your Calendar or whatever schedule you're using, then you will know the kind of article you must write, its word count, and the date each month you've got to bang out that article. It gets into a routine. Boom, the date pops up, then you get your article out.

Now that you know the secrets for planning a profit-producing newsletter, we are going to tackle the nuts and bolts of the newsletter: the design, layout, and copy. First, let's discuss design and layout, so you can begin to visualize your newsletter taking shape.

Newsletter Program Planning Form

Who will be reading our newsletter? Be specific.

What problems do they have? What do they want to know about?

What other marketing pieces of ours will they see? How will those pieces work with the newsletters?

What is our newsletter name?

What is our tagline?

How often will we mail our newsletter? I strongly suggest monthly.

What should be in every issue?

Developed by Jim Palmer - The Newsletter Guru
www.TheNewsletterGuru.com
Copyright 2009 by Custom Newsletters, Inc

Issue Planning Form

ITEM	WHO?	DUE?
Main article		
Back page article		
Other Stories		
Regular features		
Offer		
Response Mechanism		

Developed by Jim Palmer - The Newsletter Guru
www.TheNewsletterGuru.com
Copyright 2009 by Custom Newsletters, Inc

Chapter Four:
Packaging Your Newsletter:
Design & Layout

Design and layout are the "packaging" of your newsletter. Technically, "design" or "graphic design" usually refers to the things in the newsletter that stay the same. That includes the masthead, tagline, the address block (your contact information), and other things that don't change their placement, look, or content from issue to issue.

"Layout" usually refers to the arrangement of the "elements" of the newsletter on the page. "Elements" include text, pictures, captions, and graphics.

Your newsletter's design and layout affect the image that your newsletter and your company present. Your design and layout also affect how easily people can use your content and how much value they get from your newsletter. Your newsletter is an important part of your overall marketing strategy. A professional and consistent look will help present a polished and professional image of your company. At the end of this chapter there's a Checklist for Layout and Design form to help you evaluate your own newsletter.

The Mailing Panel

The mailing panel is one of the first things your customers see when they get your newsletter. It is important to put as much emphasis on the design of the mailing panel as you do the front page. One of the things that you'll see in most of my newsletter designs is what I refer to as the "horizontal aha." This is the small horizontal box above the fold and just below the address box. This is where I put a short, interesting tip or factoid that when read will cause your customers to go, "aha!" The idea is to engage them quickly, even before they break the tab and unfold the newsletter. The secret is that the sooner you engage them, the greater the chance that they'll read your newsletter.

What Draws the Eye

If you want people to look at something in your newsletter, you should present it in a way that attracts the eye. You can see examples of each of these in our samples at the end of this chapter. You should also try looking at other print publications.

Color and contrast draw the eye. A colored element on a black and white page attracts the eye. So does a thick, black border around a text box.

It isn't absolutely necessary to produce your newsletter in color. With the proper use of shading, reverse text (white text on black background), borders and bold fonts, you can design a black and white professional newsletter.

Headlines draw the eye. Decades of newspaper reading have taught us to look for headlines. We look for them to get an idea of what to read. We scan the subheads to pick up on the key points.

Position draws the eye. Without anything else to draw it, the eye comes to rest about two thirds of the way up the page and slightly to the left of center. That's a good place to put something interesting.

Pictures and graphics draw the eye. We love pictures. They may not be worth a thousand words, but pictures and graphics draw our attention. That may be why the captions on photographs are among the most-read parts of any publication.

Newsletter Guru Nugget: Pictures "sell" the story. The right choice of a picture will almost guarantee that the article will get read.

Make sure your newsletter has good quality pictures and graphics. The originals should be focused and crisp. The reproduction on the page should be the same.

Note: Do not use pictures captured from the Internet—they are 72 dpi (dots per inch) and newsletters are printed at 300 dpi. When you capture images from Web sites, they look grainy and out of focus when printed. You want your images to be crisp and clean and to compliment your article, not detract from it. Pictures sell the story, and the choice of picture will almost guarantee whether or not your newsletter article will be read.

There are many photos sources available on the Internet where you can purchase professional photographs for a few dollars—iStockPhoto.com and Fotolia.com are two sources widely used. Search their databases using keywords, and select from thousands of photos. There's bound to be at least one to compliment your article and add professionalism to your newsletter.

Size draws the eye. The largest picture, headline, or article on the page will draw the reader's attention. Devote the most space to the most important content.

Callout boxes draw the eye. Another way to grab attention is with a startling, interesting, or provocative comment in the form of a callout box. If you look at the front page of many daily newspapers, you'll see a quote of some kind or a half sentence from an article, pulled out and blown up into a large font and framed inside a box with a border. If you're using 10- or 12-point Times New Roman for the bulk of your newsletter, the font in the callout box might actually be 18- to 24-point Times New Roman. The box and contents call your attention, which is where the term "callout box" comes from. Make sure the text you put in each callout box is compelling.

Newsletter Guru Nugget: If you are only producing a two-page newsletter, print it on heavier stock such as #80. By using a heavier stock paper, the newsletter will feel like a four-page newsletter—and get the attention it deserves.

Great Newsletters Are Scannable

Someone who picks up your newsletter should be able to get the key points in any of your articles just by scanning.

Use simple subheads to highlight key points. If you have more than one key point in your text, you can use more than one subhead. That's a technique we're using in this book. Look at any chapter, and the subheads will give you an outline of the key points.

Use **boldface** to call attention to important words and phrases. Notice how your eye naturally is drawn to the boldfaced word in this paragraph.

You want to stop a scanner dead in their tracks. Because if a scanner scanning the newsletter doesn't stop and read the articles, it's not likely they're going to get a lot out of it. The whole idea is you want them to read the newsletter.

There are also devices you can use to increase readability. Charts often make concepts clear. Bulleted lists are great for summarizing key points and make newsletters crisp, clear, and easy to read.

The Secret to Selecting Typefaces

Headlines and body copy are the way that text is presented to the reader. You want your design to be both professional looking and readable. Start by fully understanding the following important terms.

A **typeface** is a style of type. This line is in a typeface called Times New Roman.

There are two basic kinds of typefaces that you'll see in great newsletters. 1) There are "**serif faces**," like Times New Roman. A "**serif**" is the little curl or footing on the letters. A **bookface** is a typeface with both serifs and shading. Times New Roman is a bookface. 2) There are also "**sans-serif**" typefaces. That means that there are no serifs on the letters. Arial, the typeface being used in this sentence, is a sans-serif typeface.

A **font** is the rendition of a letter or word in a typeface. This is Times New Roman 10-point font. **Point** is the size of the type. **This is Times New Roman 10-point Bold.**

Right now you're probably thinking, "What does that have to do with me and my newsletter?" But this is important, so stay with me.

Pick up a major newspaper and look at it. You'll notice that the newspapers and the newsletter samples at the end of this chapter all use similar typefaces. They use sans-serif typefaces for headlines. They use bookfaces for body copy.

You should too. Sans-serif typefaces are good for headlines. The eye finds it easy to stop at the end of a line. Bookfaces are good for body copy. They encourage the eye to keep moving.

Readability studies and newspaper practice over decades tell us that your newsletter readers will have an easier time reading your informational copy if you follow these same conventions.

You should also keep things simple. In the early days of desktop publishing, I saw lots of newsletters that used ten or more different fonts. I still see the occasional newsletter that uses four or five different fonts. I call that "Ransom Note Desktop Publishing."

Keep all your headlines the same size and typeface. Make your subheads in the same typeface as your headlines, but slightly smaller. Body copy should be the same all over the newsletter.

I suggest 18-point Arial for headlines and 10- to 12-point Times New Roman for copy. Headlines are often the same color type as the main color of the masthead. That creates a color theme.

The Masthead and the Tagline

We've already touched on this in Chapter Three. The masthead is the major graphic element at the top of the first page of a newsletter and includes the newsletter title.

The masthead, like other design elements, should look professional. The masthead is very likely the first thing readers will notice about your newsletter. Many companies make a mistake by using clipart or amateur, hand-drawn graphics here. Don't do that. Go for a professional design. Remember that your masthead appears on every newsletter, every month.

The masthead above is from "Information Assurance," a newsletter of the West Chester University of Pennsylvania. Using the name of the university as the newsletter name wouldn't give readers a clue about the subject of the newsletter. The name of the newsletter is part of a dynamic duo with the tagline.

The typefaces, masthead, and tagline are all design elements. They won't change from newsletter to newsletter.

Why Designers Can Be Dangerous

Graphic designers do lots of good work. But over the years I've found that some graphic designers can be dangerous to business effectiveness when it comes to newsletters.

It's not that they're bad people or that they want to lead you astray. It's just that their business is design and they generally want to do more of it. They value creativity and want to be known for being creative.

Designers can be dangerous when they confuse pretty or creative with effective. Most effective newsletter designs are professional, but they're also simple and straightforward.

Newsletter Guru Nugget: You don't want readers to notice your design. You want them to notice and rave about your content.

If your customers are saying, "What a great design!" instead of "Wow! I can use that," you've got a design that's not helping you to achieve your objectives. You need to make a change.

Designers can be dangerous when they want to create a different newsletter every time. The best newsletter design is consistent issue after issue. You get used to it and your customers get used to it. It's easier for both of you. The only person who benefits from frequent new designs is the designer.

Designers can be dangerous when they don't know how to design for readability. It's surprising to me how many people are good at graphics but either they don't know about how to design for readability or they think it doesn't matter.

Designers can be dangerous when they think that all publications are alike. Amazingly few know about the special design rules for newsletters.

If you chose a designer who does any of these things, you can have a heart-to-heart chat with him or her. If that doesn't change things, it's time for a new designer.

Take a look at the various design elements from three newsletters.

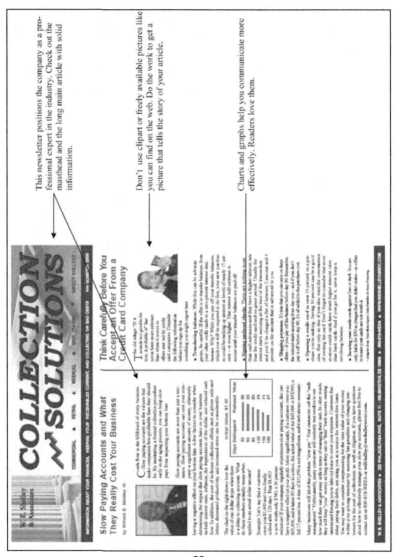

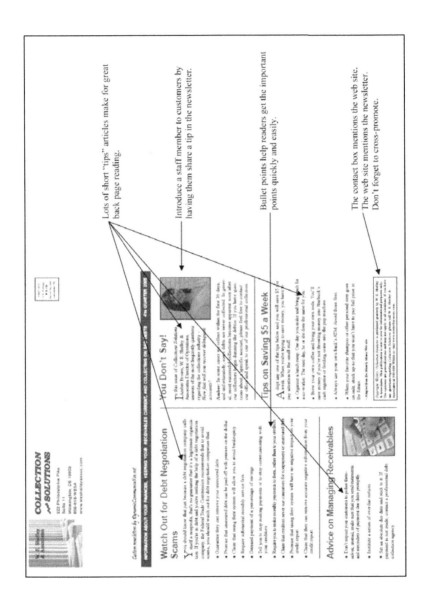

Lots of short "tips" articles make for great back page reading.

Introduce a staff member to customers by having them share a tip in the newsletter.

Bullet points help readers get the important points quickly and easily.

The contact box mentions the web site. The web site mentions the newsletter. Don't forget to cross-promote.

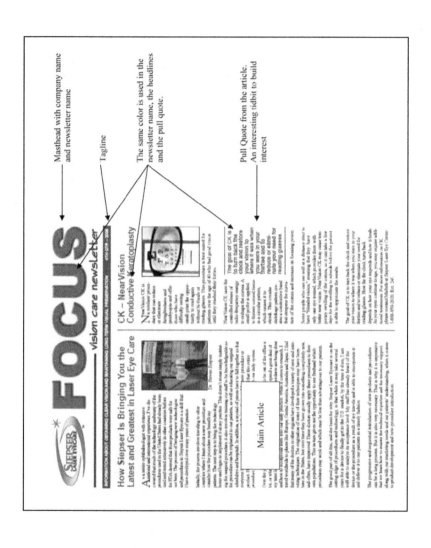

Masthead with company name and newsletter name

Tagline

The same color is used in the newsletter name, the headlines and the pull quote.

Pull Quote from the article. An interesting tidbit to build interest

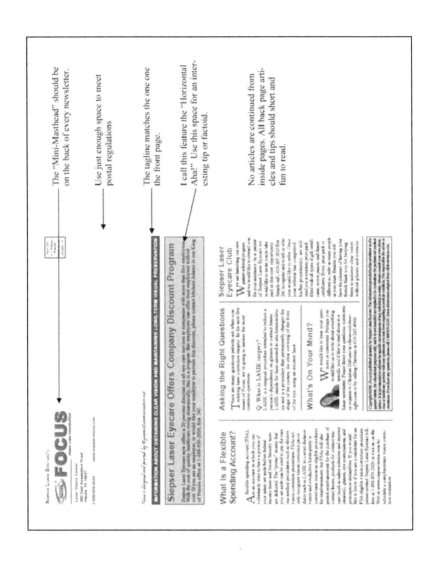

The "Mini-Masthead" should be on the back of every newsletter.

Use just enough space to meet postal regulations

The tagline matches the one one the front page.

I call this feature the "Horizontal Aha!" Use this space for an interesting tip or factoid.

No articles are continued from inside pages. All back page articles and tips should be short and fun to read.

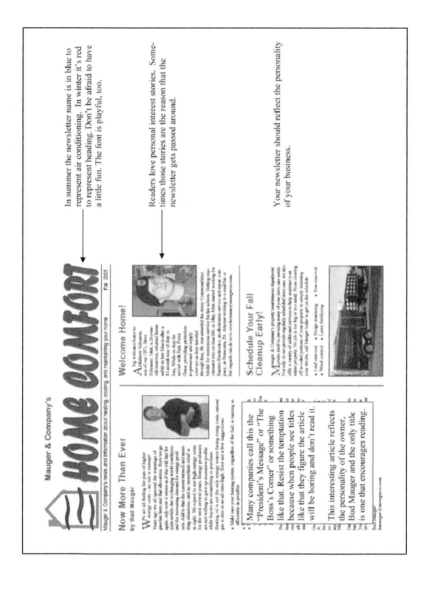

In summer the newsletter name is in blue to represent air conditioning. In winter it's red to represent heading. Don't be afraid to have a little fun. The font is playful, too.

Readers love personal interest stories. Sometimes those stories are the reason that the newsletter gets passed around.

Your newsletter should reflect the personality of your business.

The back page is prime real estate. Mauger & Company ran this short article on home generators to generate leads. They got 13 calls. Bud Mauger jokes that, "For at least a day, my newsletter was my best salesperson."

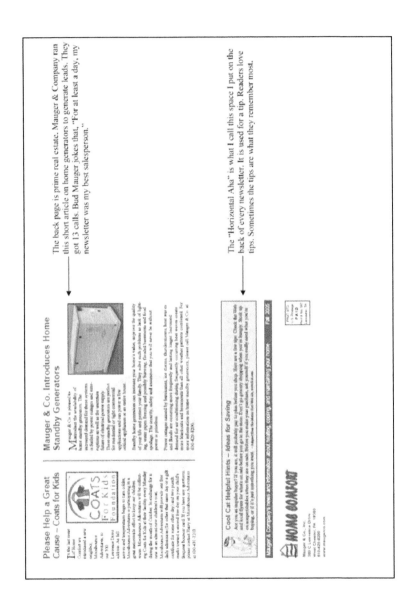

The "Horizontal Aha" is what I call this space I put on the back of every newsletter. It is used for a tip. Readers love tips. Sometimes the tips are what they remember most.

Checklist for Layout and Design

Do we have a professional masthead?

Does it include a company ID or logo?

Does the newsletter name reflect our company and our goals?

Do we have tagline that tells readers what we do?

Is there a Mini-Masthead on the back page?

Have we allowed the mailing space required by Postal regulations?

Do we have a space similar to Jim's "Horizontal Aha" for tips or key messages?

Do we have adaquate space for a main article on the front page?

Do we have adequate space for an important article on the back page?

Developed by Jim Palmer - The Newsletter Guru
www.TheNewsletterGuru.com
Copyright 2009 by Custom Newsletters, Inc

Bonus Resource: To help inspire you with your newsletter design, I'm including more than thirty cover designs in the *Bonus Resources* section in the back of the book. Many of these newsletters were designed in color. If you would like to see them in color, you can download my portfolio at www.TheNewsletterGuru.com/freebookbonuses.

Chapter Five:
Writing Copy That Sells

Good copy is the core of your newsletter. Good copy is what engages the reader and increases your sales and profits. You can have great information, but if your newsletter is not well written it won't deliver any value to your customers. Here are the factors that make great newsletter writing. At the end of this chapter you'll find a Checklist for Article Copy to help you evaluate your writing.

Great Newsletter Writing Is Readable

Most of us learned to write by writing academic papers in stiff, formal language. That might be great for college, but it won't get the job done in your newsletter.

People enjoy writing that uses a conversational tone and reminds them of conversations with a knowledgeable friend. Use words that you would use in conversations with your customer.

Don't use your special jargon or special acronyms to excess. Use words that you would use talking with a person who doesn't necessarily know your side of the industry with its special language and shorthand. Don't abbreviate except for the most common titles, names of states, and other commonly known abbreviations.

Follow the guidelines for good, clear writing. Use simple sentences. Use common words. Keep your paragraphs short.

Contractions were once considered too informal to use in a lot of marketing materials. Now the use of contractions is very standard and an accepted practice. The reason is simple. That's how you talk to somebody. For instance, replace that is with that's, you will with you'll, and so on.

Special tip: When you *do* separate words that are normally used in a contraction, you make a stronger point. For example, "This is not sold in stores." So use contractions to sound personable, and use two words instead of the contraction when you want to make a powerful statement.

Special tip: One word that has real power is the word "even," E-V-E-N, because it can add uniqueness to your offer. Consider how much weaker this statement is: "We'll refund the cost of shipping" than this: "We'll even refund the cost of shipping." Adding the word "even" makes it unique and a little more powerful, like you're doing something that other people are not.

Great Newsletter Writing Has a Personality

The whole idea behind producing a newsletter is to build rapport. Rapport is the key to getting a good response. You build rapport when you convey your personality in your newsletter writing.

Your word choice should reflect you and your common way of talking and thinking. Readers value writing with a personality, and they'll keep reading your newsletter if you provide it.

What do I mean by personality-based writing? Well, if you're a subscriber and you get my e-mails, most of those are personality-based. In my e-zine I talk about my family, the fact that my wife and I like to go kayaking, things like that. You want to share a little bit about your personality.

The best way to write conversationally is to speak directly to the reader in the first person. Use the word "you" often, and include personal examples rather than general. For example, "This month we've created a special deal just for you, our valued customer." Your customers will feel more of an affinity with copy like that, that reaches out and uses the word "you."

The opposite recommendation, by the way, is avoid writing copy with the word "I." Try to stay away from that because it's all about you. You want it to be all about your customers, Y-O-U.

Many of my corporate clients have a hard time writing with personality because they feel that if the writing isn't "professional" (i.e., stiff), then they are not conveying the proper image. But in my experience, I have found it is actually the opposite with newsletters. Customers not only want to read things that are of interest to them, but they also want to see your company in a more personable light—not a cold, corporate entity. Remember, newsletters need to be informative and fun to read, so don't be afraid to let down your corporate veil. Trade in your three-piece suit and your formal words for jeans, a cotton shirt and informal language. Write your newsletter with some personality.

Personalize with Q & A

Once I picked up a magazine called *Endless Vacation*. I was thumbing through it and began to read an article about cruises. And I said, "Oh my gosh. I've got to tell my wife about this tonight!"

They wrote the article in the form of a Q & A interview, so when I looked at the page I saw a big Q, and then a big A, and I was able to scan and pick out the questions I had an interest in.

I want to mention a couple of them specifically, because I think it will help drive the point home. The article was about ocean liners.

Talk about conversational tone and writing in a way that you would talk to somebody! It said, Question: "I've heard that crossings are often rough. Will I get seasick?" For the answer, it spoke about the massive stabilizers on board that reduce the vessel's rolling by as much as 85 percent, so even with waves as high as twenty feet you would feel little more than a comfortable rocking.

Another question was: "Uh-oh, the waves are actually getting pretty rough out here. And I'm feeling a little punk. Now what?" The writing reflects the personality of the asker, and the answer is just as personable. It discusses over-the-counter remedies and some other things you can do.

Here's the last question I'll mention. "I've never cruised because I'm afraid I'll feel trapped." The answer really made me laugh. It said, "Excuse me, but have you seen the size of these ships?"

That's a great example of drawing a reader with a conversational tone and good information, and doing so in a very entertaining way.

You can try the same. Instead of writing an article, write an interview using Q & A. You could actually do a mock interview with somebody in your office, or have somebody interview you. Simply create the questions that you want to elicit the right information for.

Great Newsletter Writing Is Short

People today are bombarded with messages and information competing for attention. Think about how you open your mail. The odds are pretty good that you do it near a wastebasket. You zip through the pile of mail, flipping most of the envelopes into the wastebasket unopened.

Then you look at what's left and you decide, "What am I going to read?" If you're like most people you'll answer that question by figuring out how long it will take to read each piece.

The magic threshold that I preach is ten minutes or less. You read things that you think will take less than ten minutes and give you value. You set everything else aside to read later. For many of us, "later" never comes.

That's how your customers work. They cull out what they think will be interesting and helpful from the mounds of incoming information.

Newsletter Guru Nugget: Great newsletters can be read in ten minutes or less.

No individual piece should take more than three or four minutes to read. Ideally each article should fit on part of a single page. On occasion it is okay to have an article continue to a different page, but don't make it continue again. This is too much work for your reader (not fun), and most readers will quickly lose interest.

Great Newsletter Writing Is Not Boring

I think it is worth re-mentioning there are some newsletter sections that, quite frankly, many people find boring. You can develop a better newsletter by simply leaving these sections out.

One of the most boring sections of a newsletter is a message from the president or chairman or some other executive message. Most of the time people don't read this section. They are usually poorly written and are not interesting to the reader. Boring. In other words, the kiss of death.

Another boring section of the newsletter is any article announcing awards won. They are usually awards from some association that your customer hasn't ever heard of (and doesn't care about). Unless it is an award that you are certain your customers will care about, it is best to leave it out of your newsletter. Remember, the goal of your newsletter is to generate new business for your company, not to bore your reader.

A really good way to bore your customers is if you write about what you do. Just as an example, if you have an automobile repair shop, and you put a newsletter out about what to check for it your car makes a certain sound, that is actually boring to your customer. Why? The reason they have a relationship with your automotive repair place is because they want bring their car to you to have it serviced. They don't want do that work themselves.

It's just like my accountant story, which I tell a lot when I speak live. My accountant sends me a newsletter. Yes, you may chuckle, he's not a client of mine, but he uses some other generic, canned newsletter. It's four to eight pages of small, 10-point Times New Roman text with very few pictures. Most of the content that he puts in the newsletter is all about the tax code and the tax law and what you need to do to avoid audits, things like that.

He comes to see me once a quarter. Once I said, "Scott, here's your newsletter." And I jokingly added, "You can save the postage." He asked, "Well, why aren't you reading it?" I said, "Because that's why I hire you. You need to know the tax code, tax laws, and how to avoid an audit. I don't."

The Magic of the AIDA Formula

AIDA is an age-old formula you may have heard of. It stands for **attention**, **interest**, **data** or **desire** and **action**. It's what I've been using to write newsletter content for years, and it truly works magic. Sometimes I'd rather just sit down, open up Word, and write on a stream of consciousness. But I've been doing newsletters long enough that I know there are certain ways you can grab attention and create interest. Bits and pieces of these topics have been touched on, but let's look at each one in a little more detail.

The first one is attention. Before you can deliver your powerful sales message, which is your article, you first have to grab the reader's attention. That's the job of the headline. A headline, combined with subheads and even pictures, is how you grab your reader's attention.

Now for the article that you write, you need to have a big, bold headline that leaves them with the feeling that says, "My gosh, I need to read this. I need to find out more!" That's the job of the headline. Your article may be fantastic, but if your headline doesn't grab them, they're not going to read the article.

A long time ago, when I managed the bicycle shop, I created a newsletter so I could sell more bike clothing. Even then I knew that I needed to create headlines other than simply the monthly special, such as *Bike Shorts $20*. People buy for two reasons—they either want to run away from pain or run toward gain. With that in mind, I created headlines based on conversations that I had with people in the store.

If you recall from the first chapter, one of the headlines that worked really, really well was, *The Secret to Riding Four Hours Instead of 40 Minutes*. The reason I chose that was because when I was talking with people on the sales floor, whether I was selling bikes or whatever, people told me, "Jim, I just wish I could ride more. Man, the seats are hard, my butt gets sore. I want to go out and get exercise, but it's just killing me." The headline evolved from there.

You can also grab your readers' attention with what's called "identification." For example, if your newsletter is highly specific and targeted, you should use the name of the group. Let me give you an example. Let's say that you are an engineer firm and you have a bunch of engineers on your subscriber list. Use the word "engineer" in the headline in some manner. Here are two examples: *Engineers, Are You Making These Three Mistakes?* or *Five Things Every Engineer Should Know About* . . . and then you can finish the sentence. If you use the name of the group that you're writing to in the headline, it causes people to stop in their tracks.

Another way to grab attention with the headline is with a benefit. A benefit is a promise to make your reader rich, or famous, or powerful, or loved, or to help save them money, or to help make them more money. It's a promise that things will be different if the reader buys your product or service.

Following are three very powerful, classic headlines. You might have read about these or heard about them if you've done any reading on copywriting. I'll break them down so you can understand how to use them in a template format.

Classic headline number one: *How I Raised Myself from Failure to Success in Selling.* If we were to make a template out of that headline so you could actually fill in the blanks as you create your own headlines, *How* is the key word. In the second blank write who the story is about or targeted to. In the third blank write how that person improved, or can improve, a certain performance.

- *How a 40-Year-Old Can Retire in 15 Years*
- *How the Next 90 Days Can Change Your Life*

So it always starts with how, and then who the article is about or targeted at, and then what the benefit is. If you use that formula, you can just fill in the blanks and can come up with some pretty cool headlines.

Classic headline number two: This headline starts with the key words *If You*. The second part of this headline is *You Can*. So *If You Are a Safe Driver, You Can Save 20% On Your Car Insurance.* In the template form write *If You*, and then in the blank put some qualification—what they need to do, who they need to be, you get the idea. Right after that, in the blank, write the benefit.

- *If You Live in Springfield, You Can Have a Free Home Inspection* Here, your business is doing home inspections, or perhaps you're a realtor.

- *If You're Over 65, You Can Qualify For Special Senior Citizen Rates*

So again—*If You*, then the qualifier, *You Can*, and then say what the benefit is.

Classic headline number three: This headline has to do with a number, followed by how to achieve something. Here's an example: *A Hundred and Sixty-One New Ways to a Gourmet's Heart*. The first part is some significant or impressive number followed by ways to achieve something good.

- *Four Ways to Keep Your Marriage Young* This may work well for someone who's a coach or a therapist.
- *Ten Ways to Keep Your Customers Coming Back* This would be a good headline on a B2B newsletter if you're a business coach or marketing coach.

So this formula is Significant Number of Ways to Achieve Something Great.

The second part of the AIDA formula is interest. So your headline has stopped the reader, and now you need to draw the reader into your article. The best way to do that is with a story. Storytelling is incredibly powerful. Stories are the way that humans have made sense of the world since we first started to speak. A short story is essential to keep your reader interested in what you have to say.

But you just can't tell any story. Your story should tell about a person who is like the reader—in other words, your target customer—who solved a problem that the reader has, and did so because of your product or service. This is a **success story**.

You need to identify with the reader and, if possible, join the conversation that's going on in their head.

That's something that Dan Kennedy and Bill Glazer have talked about for a long time. If you can join the conversation that is going on in someone's head, which typically means it has to do with a current event (such as saving money on gasoline), then you have a good way to jump in.

When writing stories, use vivid and emotional language. Powerful emotional language is not only something that's preferred in copywriting, it's essential to your success. Many people make buying decisions based on emotions. For these readers, the emotion of the story will be enough. Of course, other readers will need proof.

And again, I want to remind you that people run toward gain, and away from pain.

For example, I recently received a newsletter from my insurance company, and it really caught my attention. The headline was based on something that's very topical right now, identity theft. I do a lot of business online, so I'm always very interested in things that have to do with identity theft.

The story hooked me because I felt it was speaking to me personally. At the end of the story it told about a product, an identity theft rider that you can put on your insurance policy. To be honest with you, I never heard of that. So I called my insurance guy and said, "I got your newsletter. What's this ID thing?" And he actually said, "Jim, it's like forty bucks a year." I said, "Oh my gosh, that's an absolute no-brainer." And I almost—in a friendly way, because he's a friend of mine—chastised him. I said, "Why didn't you tell me about this when it came out? Why do I get to read it in your newsletter?" I would have signed up for that instantly. I had no idea that for about $40 a year you could get an identity theft rider on your homeowner's policy.

Ah, the magic of newsletter marketing.

It had started with a headline—something I was interested in. It told a story that related to me, and provided a solution.

Newsletter Guru Nugget: Highly effective newsletters tell, they don't sell.

The third part of the AIDA formula is data or desire. This is the place for logic. As I mentioned earlier, some people will buy based on emotion, other people on logic. Perhaps you made your case in emotional terms. Now you need to back it up with logical proof—data—so that your reader will be more comfortable taking action.

Testimonials work great here. You want to remind your customer of how you've helped him or her over the years. Or tell how long you've been in business.

You can also use an argument from authority. There are two forms. One way is to mention expert testimony that supports your claims and recommendations. The second form of authority you can use is statistics. But of all the ways you can have evidence, a testimonial is the most powerful way.

I've been counseled and coached by my mentors, Dan Kennedy and Bill Glazer, for a few years now. They agree that a poorly written testimonial from a customer is ten times more powerful than a beautifully written sales copy from you and your marketing department. People will believe other people a lot more than they'll believe you.

To build desire, reveal that you've only got a limited number or a certain amount of product you're making available for a limited time. This pushes people to make a decision.

So far we've grabbed the reader's **attention** with a powerful headline, we've drawn their **interest** into the message with compelling stories, and we've substantiated our story with some solid evidence, luring their **desire** with emotions or logical **data**. So guess what this is all leading up to? **The last A stands for action.**

All the emotional hooks and logical proof are fine. But they don't mean anything unless your reader takes action. They're more likely to do so if you *ask* them to do it. Experienced copywriters know that even if you do everything correctly up until now, you're only going to get a fraction of the responses that you want unless you ask.

I have found that this is where a lot of people drop the ball, because I read a lot of newsletters. I read a lot of newsletters because I like to get new ideas and see what other people are doing. But I'm always amazed when I'm reading a good story and it suddenly ends. I think, "Okay, what is it you want me to do?"

People skip writing a call to action for a couple reasons. Number one, they might be a little timid or shy to boldly and directly ask the customer to take action. If this is you, you need to get over this in a hurry, because if you're assuming that the reader will figure out what to do and how to go about it, you may be assuming too much. You've got to tell them what you want them to do. And you've got to lead them to do it step by step.

Bill Glazer said something in a talk once that I'll never forget. He said, "For many of us our target customer is Homer Simpson." If you picture Homer Simpson in your head when you're writing, it will do wonders, because it will enable you to simplistically write out steps one, two, and three, telling readers exactly what you want them to do. Be as specific as possible. You can't depend on them to connect all the dots. You've got to invite them to do it.

Great Newsletter Writing Is Clean

Clean writing is writing that doesn't call attention to itself. Clean writing is free of grammatical and spelling errors. Here are some tips on how to write clean copy.

Write more than one draft. Even professional writers do this. Next, sleep on it, then when you come back to a piece, it's easier to spot errors and rough phrases. It's easier to see how to improve your work.

Use your spell check, but don't make this your only spelling and grammar check. Spell-check programs are great, and you can even use them to improve your writing over time. But they can miss important things.

Spell checking programs are excellent at finding words that are spelled incorrectly. But they can't tell if a correctly spelled word is the word you meant or if it's the right word for the situation.

Here's an example of how that can get you into trouble. It comes from the humor column of a denominational magazine. The writer intended to say that people with specific business talents could "use those in the service of the church."

Alas, two letters were transposed. The spell-check didn't catch the error because the transposition still spelled a valid word. Instead, the line that went out in a letter to thousands and later caused quite a chuckle was that those people could "sue those in the service of the church."

Here's a tip for Microsoft Word users. There's a feature built into the grammar checking function that can help you improve your writing. Select the option that gives you readability statistics when you check spelling and grammar. Then every spell-check will give you two helpful statistics. 1) The Flesch Reading Ease Score gives you a measure of how easy your piece is to read. You want to make this number as high as possible. 2) The Flesch-Kincaid Grade Level measures readability in a different way. It computes the lowest grade level that can read your piece and easily understand it. You want to get this below 10 and usually above 6 for newsletter copy.

Fortunately, one of the best ways to judge the quality and readability of your writing is also one of the easiest. **Read your writing out loud.** Don't read it on your monitor. Print it out and then read it. Even better, have someone else read your piece out loud to you. Reading aloud calls attention to every rough spot and unnatural phrasing. You'll instantly discover that the way you talk out loud is not necessarily how you write, and your copy will swiftly improve. I suggest doing this for everything you write.

Get someone to edit and proofread your articles. When we look at our own writing, we usually see what we intended to write. We're likely to skip over phrasing problems and not spot errors in word usage, spelling, and typos.

There's an expression in the information marketing world: "Good is good enough, get it out there." I believe that. I don't necessarily strive for perfection. I strive for doing the best job I can. To be honest with you, I use an outside proofing company. I can send them anything. I can send them PDFs, Word documents, whatever. For a very, very reasonable fee, two English majors read over it then send it back with their comments and suggestions. It's very cheap. I think it's either $9 or $11 for a page, which is 500 words, very cheap. One of the hardest things in the world is to proofread your own stuff.

Great Newsletter Writing is Legal

The most common way newsletter editors can run into trouble is to infringe upon copyrights by illegally reprinting articles from other sources such as print publications and Web sites.

Copyright issues can easily fill an entire book, but let me just say that the only way you can legally reprint a copyrighted article in a print publication is to get permission (preferably written) from the publication in which it first appeared.

On the Internet the same rule applies, but there are two other sources of articles that you may use legally. One example is on my friend Wally Bock's Web site.

Wally gives you permission to use some of the material you find there, but he's careful to tell you which articles you can use and what you have to do. Here's the notice that appears on articles you can reprint.

"You may reprint or repost this article providing that the following conditions are met:

- *The article remains unaltered.*
- *Wally Bock is shown as the author.*
- *The notice Copyright 2007 by Wally Bock or similar appears on the article.*
- *Contact information for Wally is included with the article. You may refer readers to this Web site as a way to meet this requirement, or use the information on our contact page.*

Any other reprinting or reposting requires specific permission."

When the copyright owner sets conditions on what you need to do, you must follow those rules or you will be violating the law. If you want to do something different, you need specific permission.

There are also Web sites called "article banks" or "article distribution sites" or "free article sites." They have articles that you can reprint, but they also set conditions. You must adhere to their conditions in order to use the material legally.

The most popular of these sites is Ezine Articles. They lay out their conditions in detail at www.ezinearticles.com/terms-of-service.html. Other article sites have similar rules and restrictions.

> *Newsletter Guru Nugget:* My recommendation is simple. Don't use any material unless you're absolutely sure that you have permission. When in doubt, leave it out.

Every Issue Features Check

Your every-issue features may already be planned. They might be your most important stories, or you may have planned them for elsewhere in the issue. If not, take a moment to make sure that they'll be in this issue. Items to include in every issue are name of company, street address, phone number, Web site, and e-mail address.

Just in recapping, the reason that a friendly customer newsletter works so well is that it's filled with useful information. It teaches the reader something. Maybe it makes them laugh. It's fun and interesting. People get a good feeling when they're reading good news, because they usually read a lot of negativity. If they feel more optimistic, they're going to feel better about themselves, and they're going to feel better about you.

The Checklist for Article Copy is on the next page. Use it as a master form and copy it as needed. Use it to evaluate every article you write for your newsletter.

Checklist for Article Copy

Use this form to help evaluate every article you write for your newsletter.

Does it help the customer solve a problem or answer a question?

Does the writing have personality?

Does it reflect the values and style of our company?

Have you read this piece aloud?

Have you run a grammar and spell check?

Is the article scannable?

Is the article short?

Consider that the average American reads silently at 300 words per minute.

Do we need any copyright permissions?

Developed by Jim Palmer - The Newsletter Guru
www.TheNewsletterGuru.com
Copyright 2009 by Custom Newsletters, Inc

Chapter Six:
E-mail or Print?

Recently I ran into someone I once worked with. He knew I was in the business of helping people improve their business using newsletters. We hadn't seen each other for a long time, though, so I wasn't surprised when he said, "I guess your business is pretty much all e-mail newsletters now, Jim."

I guess that's a logical assumption. After all, the news is full of e-this and e-that, and I embrace new technology. My Web site and e-mail are an important part of my business.

But, as I told my friend, an e-newsletter can't begin to deliver the benefits that a great print newsletter can. There's a place for electronic communication in your business, but for keeping customers and getting more and building relationships, print is the choice hands down.

Advantages of Print Newsletters

Print is still the preferred way to read larger documents. Many people simply do not like to read large documents on their computer monitor.

Print also gives you total control over the look and feel of your message, which is an extremely important element of your businesses image.

Ironically, print doesn't have to compete with as much "noise" as e-mail does. Most people receive five or six pieces of mail a day compared to the fifty or sixty e-mails they receive daily.

Print newsletters are great tools for enhancing brand awareness, deepening credibility, and building customer loyalty. You can pack each of your print newsletters with in-depth articles and multiple messages—making each issue informative, fun, and easy to read.

Advantages of E-mail Newsletters

Sample of my weekly e-zine, "Jim Palmer's Fastest Way To Higher Profits!"

Conversely, electronic media such as e-mail newsletters (sometimes called e-zines or e-newsletters) are about access, speed, and convenience. The relatively low cost of producing an e-mail newsletter allows for a subtle but important difference in your marketing strategy. You can focus each e-mail newsletter on a single topic or idea, and you can deliver these messages as often as you want based on what you've determined will help you accomplish your goals.

Just like print newsletters, e-mail newsletters are also great relationship builders. A study published by the Nielsen-Norman Group showed that many readers become emotionally attached to e-mail newsletters and actually look forward to receiving them.

And unlike print, customizing content for your readers is easy and inexpensive with e-mail newsletters. Perhaps the biggest advantage of electronic media is its speed, which allows you to take advantage of opportunities as they occur. Sign up for my free weekly e-zine, "*Jim Palmer's Fastest Way To Higher Profits!*" at www.JimsNewsletter.com.

Problems with E-mail Newsletters

E-mail communication has its place. It's great for communicating to individuals and small groups. But e-mail newsletters also come with problems. Here are just a few.

The first problem you have is getting people to sign up for your newsletter. That usually means they have to go to your Web site, find the place for newsletter sign-up, and initiate the process. Not everyone is willing to do that.

Because of abuses by spammers, the best practice today is for electronic newsletters to use a double opt-in system for signing people up. When people first sign up they're sent an e-mail that says, in effect, "We want to make sure it's really you who signed up for our newsletter, so please do this."

That's followed by instructions to click on a link or reply to the message. It sounds simple, but the research of one marketing expert shows that a third of the people who sign up don't complete the double opt-in process.

That gives you a problem because you've got people expecting your newsletter who aren't going to get it. They'll think it's your fault and that you're not doing what you promised.

E-mail addresses change far more frequently than physical addresses. And when people change their e-mail address, there's no simple address change notice for them to send like there is for a physical address change. Again, you are now losing touch with your customers and clients.

All of that is a recipe for non-delivery and frustration. And you haven't even sent your new subscriber a newsletter yet.

Thanks to spammers, most companies and individuals use some kind of spam blocking and e-mail filtering software. That blocking and filtering can catch your electronic newsletter and imprison it in a junk mail folder.

If the electronic newsletter makes it to your customer's inbox there's another problem. It's called clutter.

Take your physical mail. You can scan through it quickly and throw the junk away. Envelopes look different. You can spot familiar logos and addresses and senders' names.

Not so in your e-mail inbox. There every message looks the same in an inbox filled with subject lines.

Electronic newsletters don't have the pass-along readership that print newsletters have. That means you don't have the same referral possibilities.

Your great design can be sabotaged by technology. Graphics may not make it through the spam filter. And people read their e-mail on lots of different-sized screens that can scramble the greatest layout. With print, the newsletter you send is the newsletter they get.

To sum up, e-mail newsletters lack the consistency and reliability you need to keep the customers you have and develop relationships with new ones.

E-mail newsletters can be an effective supplemental communications channel, but you have to make decisions about how you're going to do them.

Elements of a Great E-mail Newsletter

As I mentioned previously, most people receive a high volume of e-mail on a daily basis. I, myself, get over one hundred e-mails a day. With that much e-mail to deal with every day, most folks scan their e-mail to see if it is even worth reading.

The first element of a great e-mail newsletter is that it's scannable (just like print newsletters). Assume that recipients will not start at the top and read everything. Write your e-mail newsletter with headings, subheads, bullets, and short sentences, just as you would your print newsletter. You want it to be easily scanned because people are pressed for time.

If you look at copy on really good Web sites, you can scroll and easily find the bolded headlines or subheads. Simply by scrolling you get a feel for the entire article without actually reading it. That's the way to grab the scanners.

The second element of a great e-mail newsletter is to utilize the subject line to its fullest extent. There are two proven ways to handle the subject line. Some successful e-mail newsletters use the name of the newsletter as the subject line for every issue. An example would be "Your August Issue of [insert newsletter name here]."

The other successful method used is highlighting the benefit the reader will receive if they read the e-mail newsletter, such as "How to Get More Done in the Same Amount of Time." Either way is effective. Pick the method that fits best with your e-mail newsletter.

The third element of a great e-mail newsletter is to make it the right length. People rush through their e-mail. Remember, e-mail is "noise," an interruption to their day, and on average, they receive fifty or more "interruptions" on a daily basis.

If you make your newsletter too long, people will scroll down and say, "This is too long," then do one of two things with it. They may simply delete it unread. You don't want that reaction! Or they may intend to read it later, when they have time. In most instances, that time never comes and your e-mail newsletter goes unread (and eventually gets deleted). Again, this is not the desired action.

My recommendation is to keep e-mail newsletters to no longer than one thousand words. Most people can read the entire thing in about five minutes.

The final element to a great e-mail newsletter is the same as print: make it consistent, predictable. Unless your e-mail newsletter delivers breaking news, let your subscribers know when to look for it. This reduces the probability that they'll confuse your e-mail newsletter with spam. So pick a schedule and stick to it. The same day of the month, the same time of the day.

Key E-mail Newsletter Decisions

I recommend that you use an e-mail newsletter to supplement your print newsletter and other marketing efforts. To use this strategy, there are several basic decisions you have to make. The first one is which format to use.

Some e-mail newsletters are pure text. There are no graphics. There are no layout issues. These newsletters show up in an e-mail inbox looking very much like a garden-variety e-mail message.

Other newsletters make use of the formatting that an HTML allows. They use color and graphics and more active links than pure text e-mail newsletters.

Pure text newsletters are more likely to make it through spam filters. HTML newsletters are more visually interesting. Which is best? There are experts lined up on both sides. Each side has studies to support their position. My suggestion is to test things and see which format works best for your customers.

By now you might have the impression that I don't think you should use an e-mail newsletter. Nothing could be further from the truth.

E-mail newsletters are a powerful part of most marketing arsenals today. I use one myself. If you'd like to subscribe to my e-mail newsletter, just go to www.JimsNewsletter.com and enter your name and e-mail in the yellow box at the top right.

Occasionally I even step up my e-mail marketing for a specific reason. Some weeks I send e-mails almost every day. For example, I send more frequent e-mails if I have two or three different promotions taking place within a close time frame. This is another key decision you will need to make—the frequency of your e-mail contact with your customers or clients.

Be aware: Every single time you send out an e-mail, even if it's an e-zine that people subscribe to, some people will unsubscribe. That's just fine with me and it should be fine with you. It shouldn't ruffle any feathers at all. Here's why. Those are the people who are more than likely not your target customer. Those people who don't want to hear from you, or who think "oy! I've heard from you too much" are probably not going to buy from you anyway. So this is another key—you need to decide how you're going to react to this response.

I look at that two ways. One, if you're ever in sales and you read any of the sales training books from the gurus, they say that every time you get to a no you're one step closer to a yes. That's one good way to look at it. The other way to look at it is that the people who unsubscribe are self-cleansing your list.

My subscriber list does not go up and down dramatically. I'm constantly gaining new people, and whenever I launch an e-mail some people unsubscribe. An e-mail newsletter subscriber list may grow a little every week, but unless you actively market or do Google Ad-Words, don't expect it to grow a great deal.

There's a term that some of the high-end e-mail Internet marketers say: Don't be an Internet wimp.

If you want to get seen and make a difference in your bottom line, you've got to be bold and you've got to be in contact with people. Again, some people will find it a little too much and they may unsubscribe, and that's okay. You're cleansing your list, and those who remain are your target customer.

E-mail newsletters can deliver great value, as long as you don't expect them to do what a print newsletter can do. I recommend that you use both, get the benefits of both, and use them both to build your profits.

Using Print and E-mail Together

Here's how to use e-mail and print together for maximum benefit.

Every month, your print newsletter will reach your customers and prospects. If you sell to businesses, you can direct the newsletter to key decision makers.

If your print newsletter is informative, fun, and easy to read, people will look forward to it. They will read it and pass it on or copy articles to send to others. Those pass-alongs will become a source of referral business. If you also do an e-mail newsletter, be sure to promote it in your print newsletter.

If it fits your strategy and doesn't take up too much staff time, supplement your monthly print newsletter with a short e-mail newsletter to alert readers to informative articles that are in the print newsletter or on your Web site. Tell them how they can get the print newsletter if they don't already subscribe.

Send out your print newsletter monthly. Send out your e-zine twice a month. (Note: Many e-mail marketers have tested sending e-mails on different days and have determined that the best day to send an e-zine is either Tuesday or Thursday.)

Perhaps stage it so that your print newsletter hits one week and the e-zine the next week, a week off, and then your e-zine, then your print newsletter. This way you're communicating with your customers at multiple times and in different ways, maintaining that top-of-mind awareness.

Action Step: List the ways that your newsletter will improve other aspects of your marketing. Then, list ways that other marketing efforts can also promote your newsletter.

Chapter Seven: Producing Your Newsletter

When you've planned your basic newsletter program, designed your newsletter, and created the copy for your first issue, you still have choices to make. You have to decide how you're going to produce the newsletter and distribute it.

Local Printer

Local printers produce many small business newsletters. They can work well if you shop for price and if you hold the local printer to good design standards.

To make sure that will work for you, ask for references from local businesses for which the printer has done a newsletter. Then talk to the references. Discover what they think of the printer's quality and price. Ask how easy the printer is to work with and whether the printer delivers as promised.

Specialty Printer

There are specialty printers that do newsletters as their main business. They produce good quality at a good price if you have a large enough quantity.

That's the catch. Most newsletter and catalog sheet specialty printers don't start being cost effective until you get into large quantities. Not only that, many have set-up prices and short-run charges that can suck your budget dry. Be sure to ask about all charges at every level of quantity, and get everything in writing.

There's one more thing. In the Digital Age, many of these companies do their printing somewhere other than the United States or Canada. Find out where the printing is actually done. Then ask two more important questions.

Ask: "Who decides if my print job is acceptable?" The answer you want is that you decide. Get this in writing. Be clear that an acceptable job is acceptable print quality delivered on time.

Ask: "Who do I call about making good on a bad job, and what happens then?" The answer you want is that you call a local person who is responsible for making things right and that if they can't do that, you get a refund. Get this in writing too.

Newsletter Guru Nugget: Printing and mailing your newsletter is as easy as 1-2-3 with The Newsletter Guru's Concierge Print and Mail on Demand Service (www.NewsletterPrintingService.com). Get a quote today!

The "No Hassle" Newsletter Way

No Hassle Newsletters (www.NoHassleNewsletters.com) came about because of my success as "The Newsletter Guru." Here's the story.

My first company, Dynamic Communication, was growing fast. My clients were happy with what I was able to do for them, and I was having fun.

The problem was that to keep growing in the way I was, I'd have to hire employees and I didn't want to do that. I'd already been a boss, and I wanted to spend my time dealing with newsletters and clients, not being the boss of several employees.

I was also worried about quality. I was proud of the way my clients thought about me and my service. I knew that if I hired someone it would be hard to find a person with the talent and work ethic to treat my customers the way I wanted to treat them. It dawned on me that a computer could do a more consistent job than many employees would choose to do.

So after my friend and printing rep, Bobby Deraco, introduced me to a revolutionary print system, I spent nearly a year developing the technology and process that would become my second business, No Hassle Newsletters. Using my proprietary Web-based design and order system, customers nationwide (now internationally) can personalize, customize, and mail high-quality print newsletters to their customers at very low cost.

I created No Hassle Newsletters with small- to medium-sized businesses in mind, but it is also a great resource for start-ups that typically cannot afford a professional writer/designer and don't need to print and mail large quantities. In fact, the minimum quantity is only one hundred pieces. Here's how it works.

You select the newsletter template that works best for you. I've developed some that are industry-specific and have more of those in development.

There are also two non-industry-specific templates. One is for businesses that sell to businesses (B2B). The other is for businesses that sell to consumers (B2C).

The following pictures are of my two-page In Touch newsletter. Each done-for-you issue can be customized with your contact information, monthly personal message, company logo or your picture, and there is even room for your monthly special offer.

 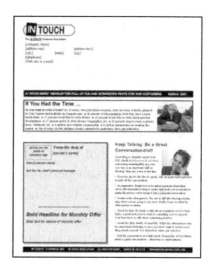

After you place your order, my No Hassle Newsletter team takes over. We produce your newsletter and either mail it for you, or send the newsletters to you for mailing. You can also order additional copies for handout, and we will ship the extra newsletters to your office.

There's nothing else like it in the world. You get a professional quality newsletter that you can add your own content to for a price you can't match elsewhere. In fact, with No Hassle Newsletters, you can customize, print, and mail a newsletter for about a buck a piece—postage included! My unique selling proposition (USP) is that "No Hassle Newsletters puts a fence around your herd in less than 13 minutes."

Make the Most of Mailing Lists

For those who have small customer lists, there are mailing list companies out there to assist you, such as Info USA and as a member or client of No Hassle Newsletters, me or someone on my staff will be happy to work with you to help you acquire such a list.

Here's a couple of different ways we can do that. In an interview we figure out who your target customer is—male or female, the average age, where they predominantly live or work, their average income, do they have kids, do they own a home, what's the value of the home, maybe sometimes what's their credit rating. Once we know everything about your perfect target customer/prospect, then I go to my list services, give them all these categories, and they come back with a list of clients in the geographic area that you specify.

There are different prices depending on whether you're getting a residential list or whether you're getting a business to business list. But I can tell you it's very reasonable.

The good news is, once you rent the mailing list you can use it multiple times. You can rent the list once, or you can mail the people time and time again. If you have any questions about it, shoot me an e-mail. I've got answers.

If another mailing list solution worked better, I'd tell you plainly. Or I'd invent it.

I recently interviewed a print and mail expert on my monthly coaching call and he shared some good tips. To listen to an excerpt of this call go to www.TheNewsletterGuru.com /freebookbonuses.

Distribution

There are two basic ways to distribute your newsletter via the U.S. Postal service. First-Class Mail is the easiest and the most expensive.

First Class is the easiest because all you need to do is stamp your addressed newsletter and send it out. If you've got the address wrong, the Postal Service will forward the mail. If you ask for an address correction, they will tell you the new address and charge you.

What used to be called Bulk Mail is now, officially, Standard Mail. It's a way to get a lower postage rate by doing some of the Postal Service's work for them. To use Standard Mail, your pieces must be essentially identical, without any personal information except the address.

The work that the Postal Service wants you to do is sorting. That sounds easy until you look at the regulations. There are also other regulations and a permit that you'll need in order to get the Standard Mail rate.

You should do your own analysis, but most small businesses find that using First-Class postage is a very small cost differential on their relatively small mailing lists. It's worth the cost differential to most of them to reap the benefits of ease of mailing and forwarding of misaddressed pieces.

Chapter Eight:
Do It All Yourself or
Outsource?

Putting it All Together

You have several tasks to complete if you want to have an effective newsletter that you can mail monthly to customers and prospects, one that helps you improve your profits. Here's a quick list.

- Create a professional newsletter design that you will use for all your newsletters
- Plan each individual newsletter, write the copy, and take the pictures
- Lay out the individual newsletter
- Check for quality
- Have the newsletter printed and mailed

This works if you have the skills, time, and resources to do a professional job at every task.

One of the downsides of creating a newsletter entirely by yourself is that each month you are responsible for 100 percent of the content and production. Trust me, having done this for many years, it is not a fun position to be in. One of the pitfalls of this predicament is when you don't know what to say, you are tempted to fill your newsletter with articles about you—company information and awards. Stuff that your readers don't care about and that doesn't add value to the relationship you are trying to build with your customers. Don't do this!

The "No Hassle Newsletter" Way

Yep, another shameless plug coming. Newsletters are what I do and what I do well.

As discussed earlier in this book, one of my most successful products is No Hassle Newsletters. Subscribers live throughout the United States, Canada, England, Australia, and The Netherlands. Every month I provide No Hassle Newsletters members with several ready-to-use newsletter templates in MS Word, so they are quick and easy to edit. Members also receive my twenty-four-page Success Advantage Newsletter and More that is filled with a wide variety of content that customers love to read, and subscribers are free to copy and paste these articles into their newsletter. I also provide a ready-to-use e-zine template, and a monthly coaching call!

Each monthly issue of the Success Advantage Newsletter and More begins with tips on how to make your newsletter better and easier to produce, and the remaining pages are filled with an incredible assortment of articles, handpicked by me. Let me share with you some of the categories that you'll find in each issue:

- Calendar items
- Work Tips
- The Work/Life Balance
- Healthy Living
- Management Tips
- Making Work Easier
- Vacation Tips
- Increase Your Tech IQ
- Learning
- Financial
- Humor
- Puzzles
- Graphics

I guarantee there is something for everyone in every issue! Every month, about thirty days prior to the issue date (i.e., you will get content for your June newsletter at the beginning of May), you will receive your No Hassle Newsletter package in the mail as a Word document as well as downloadable from the membership website. My unique selling proposition (USP) for No Hassle Newsletters is that every month "When subscribers start to produce their newsletter they are at least 90% finished!" To learn more, go to www.NoHassleNewsletters.com.

Outsource Some Parts

Outsourcing parts is how many small businesses get their newsletter out. For example, many hire a graphic designer for the basic newsletter design, and then handle copy and layout themselves. A small number seek professional help with the layout or writing of the newsletter.

The danger of this method is that the amount of work necessary to get the different tasks done and to coordinate them all may keep you from getting a quality newsletter out every month.

Outsource the Entire Process

There are companies who will take on the entire task for you. They are often expensive.

There's another danger too. Many of them produce a standard newsletter for a specific industry, such as accountants. Every accountant who subscribes to their service has the same newsletter sent to his clients with exactly the same copy and illustrations. The only difference is the contact box on the back page. These "canned" newsletters can do more harm than good, leaving an impression that your company simply took the easy road and that you're just like everyone else.

Outsource the Printing and Mailing

"How do you outsource printing and mailing? Who on earth does that?" you ask? Well, I created my Concierge Print and Mail on Demand Service to make it quick and easy for my customers and clients to get their monthly newsletters out the door and into their customer's hands. The order process takes less than five minutes, and the minimum quantity is only one hundred pieces. Because of my total volume, even the prices for small orders are exceptional! Once we receive your newsletter and mailing list, my production staff will then get your newsletters printed and mailed for you. It's that simple! You can check out this amazing service at www.NewsletterPrintingService.com.

Chapter Nine:
Ten Ways to Use Mindset to
Advance Your Business

The coffeepot has worked its magic. Whether real or imagined, the aroma of fresh, steaming French roast has lured you out of bed and is reeling you, step by step, toward the kitchen, toward the cupboard where your favorite barrel-sized mug is waiting. You're officially awake. From now until the cows come home, it's time to use your mindset to advance your business.

This chapter will briefly depart from newsletter how-to in order to provide you with a bonus: entrepreneurial general business wisdom, which I have learned through the years and now pass along to you so that you may achieve outstanding business success.

Me with author, speaker, and coach Lee Milteer. Learn more about Lee at www.milteer.com.

"How do I use mindset to advance my business?" you ask? Begin by asking questions in your mind. When you ask yourself questions, your subconscious mind starts to figure out answers, and the gears start clicking, feeding your thoughts and ideas. What you focus on consciously directs your thoughts subconsciously. It helps you develop a more positive mindset, and your "impossible" goals become possible.

I believe it is vitally important to continuously invest in your education. One way that I do that is I read three to five books per month. Among the books in my library you'll find classics such as *Think and Grow Rich* and *Psycho-Cybernetics*, and a great book by Lee Milteer, *Success is an Inside Job.*

Several of the business building philosophies and strategies that I have learned and use regularly were recently featured all together in Lee's "Smart Thinking" newsletter, and it inspired me to share them with you.

One. Focus on things that will help you to create wealth. Ask yourself, "What am I going to do to move my business forward? How am I going to add ten new clients this month?" Then continue on with your day and let your subconscious do its thing. When ideas hit, write them down. See which ones work for you, then run with them.

Two. This is on the flip side of the coin. You need to avoid negativity. There's so much negativity out there that you need to focus on what you want to create. Don't focus on what you don't want to create, such as, "What happens if I lose this client?" Shift your mindset. Be proactive in exposing yourself to good information and to things that inspire and uplift.

As I said, I read a lot. I read countless books about the success of people such as Donald Trump, and I love Dan Kennedy books. As of this publication, I'm reading a book by Howard Schultz on how he built Starbucks. It's inspiring. When I read things like that I feel inspired, and ideas start floating into my head about what I can do with my business.

Reading positive books and articles instead of reading all the lousy, negative stuff that you find in the newspapers and on various Web sites helps to create a place in your mind where beneficial ideas begin to spark.

The other part of that, which is sometimes not easy, is you need to eliminate negative people from your life. If you hang out with people who are doom and gloom, woe is me, this is horrible, what are we going to do? That is a drain on your positive mental attitude. You need to spend less time with folks like that.

Three. Have integrity with yourself. To create wealth you must have integrity with yourself. Be on guard against being manipulated by emotion, fear, and drama. If you schedule time to exercise, to complete your newsletter article, or to be creative and think of ways you're going to grow your business, then keep that appointment with yourself just like you would keep an appointment with an important client.

Four. Be creative. Acknowledge that people are still spending a lot of money on things they want and on things they need. If you're going to grow in whatever field you're in, you need to find creative ways to get to those people. Not everybody is sticking their head in the sand and hunkering down. There are people out there spending money. Use creative ways to reach those people.

Five. Some folks—and this one took me time to get under wraps—need the mindset to have the courage to act. Wealth rewards no wimps. If you're a wimp about having the courage to take action, implement, and stick your neck out there and take a risk, neither you nor your business will progress.

You must have the courage to act on your ideas and defy conventional wisdom, because conventional wisdom now tells a lot of people, "Just hunker down. Don't do anything now. Hoard your cash. Wait for the smoke to clear." More millionaires are created in tough times than any other time. Check history and you'll see that's true. If you feel you've got a good product or a good service, have courage to go out there and make it happen.

Six. Have gratitude. Gratitude is *not* something I lack. I had cancer. Quite frankly, I'm grateful to be alive. Develop the mindset of gratitude, because sometimes you have the opportunity to stare the alternative in the eye.

My outlook is very different now. Few things even get me upset. I'm grateful, as you can imagine, for every day that I have to face down whatever challenges come. Gratitude enables you to have a positive mindset where you feel like you can take on anything because you're grateful for it. You can even be grateful for the challenges. This mind shift is huge, and when you have an attitude of gratitude, good things are going to happen.

Seven. Follow up on promises. One of the biggest wealth attractants is simply saying what you will do and doing what you say. Ask yourself if there are any areas in your life or your business where you're not following up on promises. One of the things that I do, both in my personal life and especially in my business life, is if I say I'm going to do something I do it. If I say I'm going to deliver something, I always work to over-deliver.

Under-promise and over-deliver is a good strategy as long as your under-promise meets your customers' basic expectations. Then, when you over-deliver, you stand out from the competition. Do what you're supposed to do. Do it when you say you will. No surprises. That's a very simple way to seriously stand out.

Eight. Be knowledgeable. You need to be knowledgeable about how and why money moves in our economy. Money moves for value. If you have followed me for any period of time, even just the No Hassle Newsletter program, you know that since it started, I have consistently found ways to add more and more value to the program.

Money moves for value. Have your conscious mind ask your subconscious the question, "How can I provide more value to my customers?" Then go on with your day. What you'll find is that your subconscious mind starts dripping ideas into your head. You'll start thinking up possibilities. (Whenever you can, ask yourself mindset questions out loud.) Be knowledgeable. Find a mentor. Read. Overcome challenges, find solutions, and gain a winning mindset.

Nine. Deal with discomfort. Sometimes we have discomfort. We have frustration. We deal with fears—the fear of failure, fear of success. You need to be able to deal with those discomforts.

Fear holds many people back from achieving. You've got to tackle it. Nothing is better for conquering fear than taking action. Just keep taking the little steps, one at a time. Eventually you will get to where you want to be.

Ten. Embrace your leadership role. Let's face it, people look to you for guidance. You're the head of your company, the authority, the guru, the problem-solver. People, especially in this economy, do get worried. They look to others for leadership and guidance. They look to others for wisdom and confidence. This is a very, very good reason for sending out a monthly newsletter—you keep promoting yourself as the go-to resource in your industry.

Keep in mind at least 90 percent of the world are followers and as much as 10 percent of the world are leaders. Choose to be a leader. Wake up every day and ask yourself, "What am I doing to do to behave like a leader?"

To wrap it up, if you can change your negative attitudes and behaviors and adapt a mindset and strategies that set yourself apart, if you can wake up every day and embrace the challenges, if you are grateful for what you have, avoid the negativity, and surround yourself with positive people, if you take action and implement on multiple fronts, then you and your business will have an awesome ride.

Chapter Ten:
The Magic of Newsletter
Marketing

I began this book by talking about building your fence. I'm going to end in the same place.

What I'm going to tell you now should shake you to your core: If you're not in frequent contact with your customers, clients, and prospects—and by that I mean monthly contact, at a minimum—chances are very high that they will forget about you. According to statistics compiled by the Direct Marketing Association, customers lose 10 percent of their value each month if you do not keep in contact with them.

That means if you haven't done anything to keep in touch with prospects and customers, **they'll forget all about you in less than a year.** If that doesn't shake you to your core, nothing will.

Let me offer an example that I use all the time with realtors and mortgage brokers. Several years ago I refinanced my home and was actually blown away with the level and quality of service that I received. I was so thrilled that I immediately referred this company to a few friends.

But as the weeks and months went past, I actually forgot both the name of the company and the rep that helped me! I could drive to his office even now, but I cannot tell you his name or the name of the company! This happens every day to thousands of companies. Don't let it happen to yours.

If you've read through this book, you now know why newsletters are such powerful marketing tools. You know that using a print newsletter to reach your customers and prospects every month is the most valuable and cost-effective marketing tool there is. And you know how to create and distribute a newsletter that gets results.

I remember the following sentence from an interview call. I cannot remember if I said it or heard it, so I won't take credit for it—but I think it accurately describes why properly published newsletters work so well. So this will be my final "nugget" for this book.

Newsletter Guru Nugget: Great newsletters are sales letters in disguise!

My Final Word—A Little Tough Love

First, a quick review. In this book I've now shared with you the reasons why a monthly customer newsletter works so well and the magic it can do for your business, no matter what business you're in.

I've provided irrefutable proof that a newsletter can sell anything from a $20 pair of bicycle shorts to a high-dollar business investment. I've also shared with you my secrets to producing a newsletter that gets results.

So the question is, "Why publish a monthly newsletter?" If nothing I have written so far makes any sense, let me give you a little straight talk.

Not long ago I was a guest expert on a national tele-seminar. The host asked me this very question. I should tell you that I'm interviewed on a regular basis and I was fully prepared to give my usual answer supported with statistics and evidence, much like you've read in this book. However, on this occasion I chose to answer the question somewhat differently. It may have been at the end of a long day, or perhaps I had answered this question so many times before, I simply wanted to give a different answer. After I said it, I liked the way it sounded. So if nothing else you read about in this book has resonated with you so far, this answer is for you.

"Why publish a monthly newsletter?" ***"Because it's the right thing to do!"*** Just like changing the oil in your car every three thousand miles. It's the right thing to do. When you change the oil in your car, you don't see or feel any immediate gratification—you do it because it will make your car last longer and serve you better. It's like that with a newsletter. You publish a newsletter every month because it's the right thing to do for your business. Most of the time you won't see any immediate gratification. Customers may not mention that they like your newsletter, and you may not hear your cash register ring more often immediately after mailing it. But it is the right thing to do for your business.

Here's what I know about newsletter marketing from almost thirty years of experience. The companies that publish a monthly newsletter, month in and month out like clockwork, will have stronger, longer lasting relationships with their customers and clients. And, as history has shown, they will have more repeat and referral business. Publishing a monthly customer newsletter is simply the right thing to do.

So there you have it—I can't say it any more clearly! I'm truly happy to share what I've learned about what I constantly refer to as the magic of newsletter marketing.

Now it's up to you. Only you can take action to get and keep more customers now. Only you can take action to build healthier, stronger relationships with your customers, clients, and prospects and boost your profits by doing more repeat and referral business. Now go do it!

I wish you much newsletter marketing success!

About the Author – Jim

Learn More About Jim:

Jim's books:

The Magic of Newsletter Marketing—The Secret to More Profits and Customers for Life

Stick Like Glue – How to Create an Everlasting Bond with Your Customers So They Stay Longer, Spend More, and Refer More!

The Fastest Way to Higher Profits – 19 Immediate Profit-Enhancing Strategies You Can Use Today

It's Okay to Be Scared But Never Give Up (with Martin Howey)

Stop Waiting For it to Get Easier – Create Your Dream Business Now

Get Jim's Books At
http://www.SuccessAdvantagePublishing.com

About the Author

Check out Jim's wildly popular Smart Marketing and Business Building Programs:

No Hassle Newsletters – www.NoHassleNewsletters.com

No Hassle Social Media – www.NoHassleSocialMedia.com

Newsletter Guru TV – www.NewsletterGuru.TV

Stick Like Glue Radio – www.GetJimPalmer.com

Jim's Concierge Print and Mail on Demand Program – www.newsletterprintingservice.com

Double My Retention – www.DoubleMyRetention.com

Custom Article Generator - www.customarticlegenerator.com

No Hassle Infographics - www.nohassleinfographics.com

Jim's Mastermind and Private Coaching – www.TheNewsletterGuru.com

The Magnetic Attraction and Retention System (MARS Training Program) – www.MarsTrainingProgram.com

Jim's Free Weekly Newsletter – www.JimsNewsletter.com

Interested in hiring or learning more about Jim? Visit www.TheNewsletterGuru.com

About Jim

Jim Palmer is a marketing and business building expert and host of Newsletter Guru TV and Stick Like Glue Radio. He is known internationally as 'The Newsletter Guru' – the go-to resource for maximizing the profitability of customer relationships. He is the founder and President of Custom Newsletters, Inc., parent company of No Hassle Newsletters, No Hassle Social Media, The Newsletter Guru's Concierge Print and Mail on Demand, Magnetic Attraction and Retention Training Program (MARS), Success Advantage Publishing, Double My Retention, No Hassle Infographics, and Custom Article Generator.

Jim is the acclaimed author of

- *The Magic of Newsletter Marketing – The Secret to More Profits and Customers for Life*
- *Stick Like Glue – How to Create an Everlasting Bond With Your Customers So They Spend More, Stay Longer, and Refer More*
- *The Fastest Way to Higher Profits – 19 Immediate Profit-Enhancing Strategies You Can Use Today*
- *It's Okay To Be Scared – But Don't Give Up* – A book of hope and inspiration for life and business
- *Stop Waiting for it to Get Easier – Create Your Dream Business Now!*

Jim was also privileged to be a featured expert in *The Ultimate Success Secret*; *Dream, Inc.*; *ROI Marketing Secrets Revealed*; *The Barefoot Executive*; and *Boomers in Business*.

About the Author

Jim Palmer speaks and gives interviews on such topics as newsletter marketing, client retention, entrepreneurial success, the fastest way to higher profits, how to use social media marketing and how to achieve success in business.

Jim is a cancer survivor, has been married for thirty-three years, and has four grown children and a grandson. He lives in Chester County, Pennsylvania with his wife, Stephanie, their cat, Linus, and Toby, the marketing dog. Jim and Stephanie love to kayak, travel, and spend time with their family.

Connect with Jim on Facebook, Twitter, Google+, LinkedIn®, and tune into his Web TV show.

For more resources and information on Jim, his blog, and his companies, visit www.NewsletterGuru.tv.

To get your copy of Jim's free weekly newsletter, *More Profits and Customers for Life,* visit www.JimsNewsletter.com.

Get Coached by Jim!

Jim offers private one-on-one coaching for entrepreneurs and small business owners who want to grow a more profitable business faster.

<u>Short Term 'Fast Track' Private Tele-Coaching</u>
Jim offers a 3-month Fast Track Private Coaching Program that consists of three monthly one hour private one-on-one coaching calls and some e-mail follow up. The fee is $2750 prepaid before the first call. Calls are recorded.

<u>Annual Private Tele-Coaching (Monthly Calls)</u>
One 30-minute monthly private coaching call –
$497/month

<u>Strategic Business Consulting/Coaching Day</u>
During this unique one-day critique of your business, Jim will reveal hidden opportunities and pitfalls in your current business and marketing strategies. This dynamic one-day meeting is approximately 50% diagnostic and 50% prescriptive (ideas, strategies, and game plan to grow your business). Current investment: $10,000 in Philadelphia.

www.TheNewsletterGuru.com (see coaching/mastermind)
(Rates may change after printing. Consult web site for current rates.)

Free Marketing and Business-Building Information Reveals the Secret to Boosting Your Profits Now!

Get immediate access to valuable marketing and business-building information that will help you significantly boost your profits by getting more repeat and referral business!

- **TWO CHAPTERS FREE:** Get the first 2 chapters of three of my hit books: *The Magic of Newsletter Marketing, Stick Like Glue,* and *The Fastest Way to Higher Profits!*
- **FREE PROFIT BOOSTING VIDEO:** "The Power of Zero" will show you how to explode the growth of your business!
- **FREE MONEY MAKING REPORT:** "Don't Be A Newsletter Pansy, aka Use Newsletters And Grow Rich!"

The Newsletter Guru's Bonus Resource # 1

To help inspire you with your newsletter design, I'm going to share with you more than thirty of my newsletter designs. Many of these newsletters were designed in color.

Philadelphia AMA — Professional Marketer

EMPOWERING MARKETERS THROUGH INFORMATION, EDUCATION, RESOURCES, AND RELATIONSHIPS   APR/MAY – 2005

SALES & MARKETING

INTEGRATING SALES AND MARKETING

An Idea Whose Time Has Come

By Eric A. Gimbal

It is generally understood that sales and marketing, like oil and water, don't mix. The stories abound in every industry about the the distance between the two organizations – cold, distant silos isolated one from each other. But is that the way it must always be?

After all, they say that change is the one constant in our lives. So why can't this change too? Maybe it's time to rethink how sales and marketing can work together and consider what their collective mission should be.

There are significant advantages to integrating sales and marketing:

- Generate increased, sustainable revenue over years.

- Develop a competitive advantage that cannot easily be copied by the competition.

- Increase organizational efficiency and effectiveness, affording more opportunities for customers to be heard.

- Deliver relevant and consistent customer messaging at all times.

- Improve employee morale.

The Source

News from the Board
By Michael F. Stara, President

As a professional marketing organization, we have to practice what we preach. That means that we have to take seriously the way we brand and market our organization to our members and to the public. I'm fortunate that I have a great group backing me in this endeavor.

You have probably noticed a change in the way we are marketing lately. Here are some of the things we have been doing:

▶ Developing a consistent brand image for the Philadelphia chapter.

▶ Trying to develop multiple "touch points" to our members. We have been doing more calling and utilizing this professional newsletter, in addition to our e-mails, postcards, and Website contacts, to reach members like you.

▶ Reducing the number of e-mails our chapter sends out, but ensuring that those we do send have a higher, more professional content level.

▶ Underscoring the value we offer our membership through great programs, educational opportunities such as Marketing Boot Camp and the networking April 25-26, networking functions, and the www.marketingpower.com Website.

▶ Cosponsoring such high-profile, important annual events as the Philadelphia Innovation Conference (February 23), the AMA Mid-Atlantic Regional Marketing Conference (May 2-3), and the Philadelphia Marketing Expo (May 10-11).

▶ Increasing PR activities to enhance our image in the business community.

▶ Stressing accountability to our members. At fiscal year-end, I will report to you on our progress for the year.

Many of you responded to our February volunteer drive, during which we identified 43 new committee volunteers. Special thanks goes to Alyse Bodine, VP of Creative Talent, for organizing such an enormously successful drive, and to the board members who made the calls. I hope that the new volunteers find their assignments rewarding and educational. Through teamwork, we have and will continue to accomplish great things here in the Philadelphia chapter.

Don't miss the Philadelphia Marketing Expo May 10 and 11.

Looking forward, we intend to develop special interest groups (SIGs) to bring people of common industries together to discuss marketing issues as well as the development of a new Marketing Executive Roundtable initiative. Stay tuned!!

I always welcome your suggestions and comments about how we can do a better job of marketing to our members and prospects, since you, too, are among our region's top marketers. Feel free to contact me at president@amaphiladelphia.org.

AMA BOOT CAMP

REINFORCE AND FOCUS YOUR MARKETING SKILLS

In today's ever-changing marketplace, businesses need their marketing professionals to understand the basics of marketing now more than ever. Business is rapidly changing, and needs have increased competition faster than ever imagined. To help reinforce and focus your own marketing skills, the AMA introduces this highly interactive program facilitated by an experienced AMA instructor. Register now for the Marketing Boot Camp, and provide your

continued on page 7 ... see AMA Boot Camp

American SecuriComm's

Security Alert

NEWSLETTER

INFORMATION ABOUT LOSS PREVENTION, SURVEILLANCE SYSTEMS AND CREATING SECURE ENVIRONMENTS · OCTOBER - 2005

Enhanced Security Package Designed for Gas and Convenience Stores

Lorem ipsum dolor sit amet, consectetuer adipiscing elit, sed diam nonummy nibh euismod tincidunt ut laoreet dolore magna aliquam erat volutpat. Ut wisi enim ad minim veniam, quis nostrud exerci tation ullamcorper suscipit lobortis nisl ut aliquip ex ea commodo consequat. Duis autem vel eum iriure

dolor in hendrerit in vulputate velit esse molestie consequat, vel illum dolore eu feugiat nulla facilisis at vero eros et accumsan et iusto odio dignissim qui blandit praesent luptatum zzril delenit augue duis dolore te feugait nulla facilisi. Lorem ipsum dolor sit amet, consectetuer adipiscing elit, sed diam nonummy nibh euismod tincidunt ut laoreet dolore magna aliquam quis

Lorem ipsum dolor sit amet, consectetuer adipiscing elit, sed diam nonummy nibh euismod tincidunt ut laoreet dolore magna aliquam erat volutpat. Ut wisi enim minim veniam, quis nostrud exerci tation ullamcorper suscipit lobortis nisl ut aliquip ex ea commodo consequat. Duis autem vel eum iriure dolor in hendrerit in vulputate velit esse molestie consequat, vel illum dolore eu feugiat nulla facilisis at vero eros et accumsan et iusto odio dignissim qui blandit praesent luptatum zzril delenit augue duis dolore te feugait nulla facilisi. Lorem ipsum dolor sit amet, consectetuer adipiscing elit, sed diam nonummy nibh euismod tincidunt ut laoreet dolore magna aliquam erat volutpat. Ut wisi enim ad minim veniam, quis nostrud exerci tation ullamcorper suscipit lobortis nisl ut aliquip ex ea commodo consequat.

Lorem ipsum dolor sit amet, consectetuer adipiscing elit, sed diam nonummy nibh euismod tincidunt ut laoreet dolore magna aliquam erat volutpat. Ut wisi enim minim veniam, quis nostrud exerci tation ullamcorper suscipit lobortis nisl ut aliquip ex ea commodo consequat. Duis autem vel eum iriure dolor in Lorem ipsum dolor sit amet, consectetuer adipiscing elit, sed diam nonummy nibhat. Ut wisi enim minim veniam, quis nostrud exerci tation ullamcorper suscipit lobortis nisl ut aliquip ex ea commodo consequat. Duis autem vel eum iriure dolor in Ut wisi enim minim veniam, quis nostrud exerci tation ullam-

Escalating Gas Prices Increasing "No Pays"

Lorem ipsum dolor sit amet, consectetuer adipiscing elit, sed diam nonummy nibh euismod tincidunt ut laoreet dolore magna aliquam

erat volutpat. Ut wisi enim ad minim veniam, quis nostrud exerci tation ullamcorper suscipit lobortis nisl ut aliquip ex ea commodo consequat. Duis autem vel eum iriure dolor in hendrerit in vulputate velit esse molestie consequat, vel illum dolore eu feugiat nulla facilisis at vero eros et accumsan et iusto odio dignissim qui blandit praesent luptatum zzril delenit augue duis dolore te feugait nulla facilisi. Lorem ipsum dolor sit amet, consectetuer adipiscing elit, sed diam nonummy nibh euismod tincidunt ut laoreet dolore magna aliquam quis

Lorem ipsum dolor sit amet, consectetuer adipiscing elit, sed diam nonummy nibh euismod tincidunt ut laoreet dolore magna aliquam erat volutpat. Ut wisi enim minim veniam, quis nostrud exerci tation ullamcorper suscipit lobortis nisl ut aliquip ex ea commodo consequat. Duis autem vel eum iriure dolor in Lorem ipsum dolor sit amet, consectetuer adipiscing elit, sed diam nonummy nibhat. Ut wisi enim minim veniam, quis nostrud exerci tation ullamcorper suscipit lobortis nisl ut aliquip ex ea commodo consequat. Duis autem vel eum iriure dolor in Lorem ipsum dolor sit amet, uis autem vel eum iriure dolor in Lorem ipsum dolor sit

American SecuriComm · Corporate Office 450 Copper Drive · Newport, DE 19804 · 877-730-CCTV (2288) · www.aseur.com

THE AMERICAN FLYER

NEWS AND INFORMATION FROM THE PREMIER WHOLESALE DISTRIBUTOR OF HEATING AND AIR-CONDITIONING EQUIPMENT   2ND QTR 2007

New Business Concept – AirAdvice

American Air Distributing, Inc., is proud to offer American Standard dealers the AirAdvice monitoring system. AirAdvice is an indoor air quality monitoring system that measures temperature, humidity, CO, CO_2, particulates and VOCs. Beyond that, it is a business tool to help you generate more leads, close more sales and differentiate yourself from your competition.

It also provides a means to "level out" the busy and slow seasons. AirAdvice prints out "Smart IAQ" reports for homeowners AND recommends the appropriate products to improve conditions, based on the results of the report. AirAdvice offers a powerful means to help dealers quickly grow into strong players in the IAQ market.

Health, Comfort & Safety Analyses

Large, easy-to-read graphs

Continuous readings, 24 hours/day

For more information on how to get involved with the AirAdvice partnership, please contact your territory manager.

American Air Trip News

St. Thomas, U.S. Virgin Islands – January 22–27, 2008
- Six days/five nights at the Wyndham Sugar Bay Resort & Spa
- Round-trip flights from Philadelphia to St. Thomas
- All-inclusive plan, including meals and beverages on property
- Gala at the mountaintop restaurant Great House

Maui, Hawaii – January 29–February 4, 2009
- Seven days/six nights at the Sheraton Maui Resort at Ka'anapali Beach
- Round-trip flights from Philadelphia to Maui
- Breakfast each day, welcome dinner with open bar, two "dine-around" dinners and a luau and dinner at the Hyatt Regency
- Remember, you may carry over one year's worth of unused points. If the Maui trip is your trip of a lifetime, you may choose not to go to St. Thomas and to carry that year's points over to the Maui trip. MAF point statements are mailed monthly to help you keep track of your points. The higher the efficiency of the equipment you are installing, the higher the points that accrue – so make sure you are offering high-efficiency options to your customers.

American Air
DISTRIBUTING, INC.

IN THIS ISSUE

800-830-0853

SYMMETRY

People and Process — Balanced for Success

MARKETPLACE EXCELLENCE THROUGH WORKPLACE COMPETENCE — THIRD QUARTER 2005

ON BALANCE

Executive Coaching – If Your Employee Is Important Enough, Do It Right!
by Andy Hartnett

In the past, executive coaching was typically meant for those men and women already in senior-level positions. However, in recent years executive coaching has become a developmental step for those being prepared for greater responsibility and executive positions. Executive coaching, which focuses on such skills as communication, leadership, and management, has emerging return-on-investment data, which indicates that business coaches can lead to greater productivity and sizeable financial gains for companies. A 2004 study showed that personal coaching returned $7.90 for every $1 spent, according to MetrixGlobal.

At Symmetry Consulting, our experience shows that when executive coaching is attached to a specific project or task, superior results are achieved. The project provides the context for the coaching, immediate feedback on new behaviors, and, if successful, moves the organization forward.

Since there are no accepted standards of performance in the field of corporate coaching, there is some concern that unqualified people may present themselves as executive coaches. People who lack proper training can actually reduce the efficiency of an organization. As with any consultant agreement, the organization should first establish the business case and expectations for the coaching, and then identify the best person to achieve the business case.

If your employee is important enough to provide coaching, he or she is important enough to find the right coach. The following are a few things to look for when searching for an executive coach:

- ✔ Previous coaching experience specific to your situation (ask for references
- ✔ Business experience – to help enhance executives, the coach must know the client's world
- ✔ Certification (in its infancy) – does not replace asking good questions
- ✔ A well-defined coaching model and process

Hiring an executive coach is a key business decision, and as with any business decision, if it is made in haste, or without the right analysis, it can produce detrimental results. To learn more about executive coaching and how it can help increase the overall effectiveness and efficiency of your company, please call me at 1-866-270-7306 or email me at andy@symmetryconsulting.org.

Tool Kit: Mastering the Change Curve

It's clear – recurring change is the norm in organizational life today. Still, most of us have difficulty dealing with it. Experts in the field of change management, Drs. Dennis Jaffe and Cynthia Scott describe change as a natural progression through four phases. To successfully master change, individuals must pass through all four phases: denial, resistance, exploration, and commitment. In their book, Mastering the Change Curve, Drs. Jaffe and Scott uncover individual reactions to change and provide an understanding of how behavior affects success.

Learning Outcomes
- Gain an understanding of the four phases of change
- Pinpoint the current stage in the transition process
- Identify productive and nonproductive change behaviors
- Develop a strategy to master change

Theory
Drs. Jaffe and Scott are experts in the field of change management. The authors describe change as a natural progression through a series of four phases: denial, resistance, exploration, and commitment. To successfully deal with

continued on page 3 ... see Tool Kit

Future Focus

Coming in future issues of *Symmetry*:

Interviewing future staff with your corporate culture in mind

NEWS IN BLOOM

BLUE MOON FLORIST'S NEWSLETTER   SPRING 2004

When Dreams Come True!

Once in a Blue Moon, dreams do come true. For Ami Trost, owner of Blue Moon Florist in Downingtown, Pa., her dream of owning her own floral business came true for her at the age of 24. As a teenager, Ami intended to pursue a career in law. However, by the age of 15, her dream segued into a vision of herself as an entrepreneur and florist. While in high school, Ami worked part-time and weekends at a small, family-owned floral shop in Downingtown. Ami credits her early experiences at this establishment for her passion for the business. She was inspired by the customer interaction, the opportunity for creativity and the pleasure of working with beauty every day.

After graduating from high school, Ami worked with a select group of florists in Chester County. Ami honed her craft and expanded her design skills and experience working full time as a floral designer while studying business administration and attending evening classes at Penn State. In 1995, Ami purchased Blue Moon Florist in Guthriesville, Pa.

At that time, Guthriesville, located in East Brandywine Township, was considered a remote area in the ever-growing region of the county! This small but charming storefront shop quickly became a local favorite and for many customers a frequent stop during the day or on the way home from work. Blue Moon is open seven days a week and remains open until 7 PM on weekdays. These hours of operation are unusual in the industry. However, Ami believes in accommodating the wide-ranging needs of Blue Moon's customers by providing exceptional, personalized service. Ami and the Blue Moon team are proud to have served the community for the past

Continued on page 2 ... see "Dreams"

IN THIS ISSUE

The Power of Flowers

Flowers are not only a joy to behold, they enrich our lives in a variety of ways. For centuries, plants and flowers have been a source of food and medicine. Herbal remedies abound. Fresh flowers provide beauty to our environment and impart documented health benefits as well.

Recent research by the Society of American Florists indicates that flowers are a natural and potent mood elevator and can provide long-term health effects. The research showed that people experience a sense of happiness and excitement when they receive flowers. Flowers enhance self-esteem and restore mental acuity. Studies have shown that the presence of plants and flowers reduces stress, refreshes memory, lowers blood pressure and improves communication skills. Post surgical patients who received flowers recovered more quickly than their counterparts and senior citizens reported a marked decrease in depression following the receipt of flowers and scored higher on memory tests.

Flowers are a symbol of sharing and promote improved personal connections and increased communication skills. The presence of fresh flowers in public areas of the home or office, such as foyers and meeting rooms, create a welcoming atmosphere. Plants bring nature indoors while improving air quality by providing oxygen. Men and women alike respond positively to flowers. Sending a gift of beautiful fresh flowers is a warm and caring way to express your feelings for any occasion. Remember, you are not only brightening the day for someone special, you're also boosting his or her health, tranquility and sense of well-being. Flowers are a natural pick-me-up – pick some up today!

Now You Can Shop Online 24-7!

Blue Moon Florist is now online with a full-service Web site. Order and ship flowers anywhere and find answers to all of your flower and plant care needs. In addition, you can get many great decorating ideas by scanning hundreds of photographs. Visit the Web site at

www.bluemoonflorist.com.

the VOICE

CHESTER COUNTY CHAMBER

of Chester County Business

JAN/FEB - 2005

2003 HONORABLE MENTION AWARD

EXPO & WEB UPDATE

Expo 2005 will be held at the United Sports Training Center in Thorndale, Wednesday, April 13, 2005. We are working with John Holt and Kim Basner on the EXPO and will have room for all EXPO events including the luncheon, networking and larger booth spaces. EXPO booths are on sale now; early bird rate is $510 for Chamber Members until February 28th. All booths must be paid in advance. Last year's EXPO was the best show ever - don't miss this one!

Watch for the Chamber's newly constructed Web site to appear at the end of the first quarter with advertising opportunities, links and more! The new site will be worth waiting for! If your company is interested in marketing on the Web site and want to be the first to claim the best pages, contact Pam Jaccard for details. The site is the next phase of the Chamber's communication and marketing plan, which will unfold over the next few months. We want you to be seen on the Net!

Member Spotlight

Wawa is an amazing local success story, and for the first time in its 40-year history, the company has appointed a CEO who is not a member of the founding Wood family. The Chester County Chamber of Business and Industry is pleased to put to the spotlight on this dynamic company and it's new CEO, Howard Stoeckel.

Most recently the president and COO, Howard became the CEO on Jan. 1, 2005, replacing Richard D. Wood Jr., who will stay with the company as the non-executive chairman, and continue to provide governance and an overall strategic role. "No one replaces Dick [Wood]," said Howard. "With the way we're structuring the business, Dick, [president] There DuPont, who is Dick's nephew, and I will partner in taking the company into the future."

Wawa has made significant changes in the last few years, such as installing gasoline pumps and deciding to focus on Wawa

proprietary-branded products. "We're still early on in executing those decisions and I see no change in direction strategically, other than constant refinement of what we've been doing the last couple years," said Howard.

Howard Stoeckel

Continued on page 5... see WAWA

Quite a Crowd at 2004 Small Business Dinner!

The room was packed with smiles and the laughter of a record 340 guests at the 2004 Small Business Dinner, held November 10th at the Desmond Hotel. Citizens Bank presented the awards celebration keynote speaker Garo Yepremian, who enchanted the crowd with humorous tales of his life in the NFL and being an American citizen.

For their tireless commitment to excellence and solid community leadership, Donna Coughey, President/CEO of First Financial Bank, and Dr. Alan Elko, Superintendent of the West Chester Area School District, were honored as the 2004 Small Business Leader of the Year and the recipient of the J. Larry Boling Award for Excellence in Government, respectively. Additionally, Wegman's supermarket in Downingtown

Continued on page 5... see Business Dinner

(left to right) Chamber President Rob Powelson, First Financial Bank President/CEO, Donna Coughey and Chamber Board Chairman Tom Fillippo.

Imagine a bank where you can *Expect the Extraordinary* ◆ **First Financial Bank**

Special Holiday

NEWSLETTER

GREENHOUSES ● GARDEN CENTERS ● NURSERY ● LANDSCAPING ● WATER GARDENING ● DESIGN & GIFT

INFORMATION ABOUT HOLIDAY PLANTS, DECORATING, SPECIAL EVENTS, GIFT IDEAS AND NEW TRENDS   CHRISTMAS 2005

Merry Christmas

As we approach the Christmas season, all of us at Esbenshade's Garden Centers would like to thank you for your business. We truly appreciate the opportunity to serve you. Christmas is a special time; it is a holiday when many people give gifts to express their love and appreciation. As a Christian-based company, we also know that Christmas is the season to celebrate the birth of Jesus Christ, the greatest gift of all. With this same spirit of giving, Esbenshade's is committed to refining our marketing efforts in 2006, so that we can give more back to our customers. In sharing the benefits of this effort, you'll continue to receive the exceptional customer service you've come to expect from us, as well as the highest quality plants and products, but at lower prices. That is our gift to you. Look for more details in the months ahead. On behalf of all of our employees, I want to extend our warmest wishes for a Merry Christmas and a Happy New Year.

Terry Esbenshade

IN THIS ISSUE

Holiday Evening of Joy!

Please join Esbenshade's on **Friday, November 25, 2005** for a special holiday evening of joy as we ring in and celebrate the sights, sounds and scents of the holiday season.

Horse-Drawn Wagon Rides Visit our **Mohnton location** from 6:00 to 8:00 pm on Friday, November. 25, for a fun horse-drawn wagon ride.

Christmas Railway – Visit our **Lititz location** to see 4-G scale trains and 200 feet of track winding through a beautiful holiday setting. The trains will run all day on November 23, 25 and 26.

Live Nativity Scene – Visit our **Fleetwood location** to see a live nativity scene from 6:00 to 9:00 p.m. on Friday, November 25. The nativity scene is compliments of the Reading Calvary Church of the Nazarene.

Enjoy These Festivities at Each Location

● Dazzling display of luminaries ● FREE roast-your-own hotdogs!

● FREE refreshments (popcorn, candy canes, apple cider, hot coffee, and cookies)

● Seasonal music: Mohnton - acoustic trio; Lititz - harpist; Fleetwood - live vocal and keyboard soloist

The Beautiful Christmas Flower!

Stop in to visit our breathtaking display of poinsettias!

Esbenshade's grows more than 370,000 poinsettias in a variety of colors and sizes. You'll find red, pink, white, marble, winter rose and several special new varieties of poinsettias throughout our greenhouses. We also offer the local favorite, rose in the snow.

Lower prices all season long on our best-selling sizes
● Jumbo Single Bloom – $1.99
● Multi-Branched Poinsettia 3-4 Blooms 4.5" Pot – $2.99
● Our Best Value – Growers Special, Multi-Branched Poinsettia 4-5 Blooms 6.5" Pot – 2 for $10.00
● Great discounts on Churches poinsettias orders! Call for details.

Your Company Name Here presents

Good Housecleaning

A "GOOD NEWS" NEWSLETTER FULL OF FUN AND INTERESTNG FACTS FOR HOME OWNERS   APRIL 2007

Hello *[customer name]!*

This issue of *Good Housecleaning* is being sent to you courtesy of

two fines available for company name and/or sender's name

It is our way of saying that you are important to us and we truly value your business. Please feel free to pass this newsletter on to friends and neighbors. Enjoy!

Funny Bone

You Know You're Having a Bad Day When...

1. You wake up facedown on the pavement.

2. You see a 60 Minutes news team waiting in your office.

3. Your birthday cake collapses from the weight of the candles.

4. You turn on the news and they're showing emergency routes out of the city.

5. Your twin sister forgot your birthday.

6. Your car horn goes off accidentally and remains stuck as you follow a group of Hell's Angels on the freeway.

7. Your boss tells you not to bother taking off your coat.

8. The bird singing outside your window is a buzzard.

9. You wake up and your braces are locked together.

10. You walk to work and then find that the back of your dress is stuck in the waistband of your pantyhose.

– Adapted from the Comedy Central Web site

On Active and Passive Voice

Do you understand the difference between active and passive voice? If not, don't panic, most people would have trouble defining them or coming up with good examples.

But Stephen King, the yarn-spinner of horror who has been giving us the creeps for years, explains it clearly in his book On Writing.

Verbs, he says, come in two types-active and passive. "With an active verb, the subject of the sentence is doing something. With a passive verb, something is being done to the subject of the sentence."

King suggests avoiding the passive voice whenever possible. King says he believes that some writers are drawn to the passive voice because they believe it lends their writing some type of authority or even majesty-and that makes them feel safe.

Here are some of King's examples:

Passive: The meeting will be held at seven o'clock.

Active: The meeting's at seven.

Passive: My first kiss will always be recalled by me as how my romance with Shayna was begun.

Active: My romance with Shayna began with our first kiss. I will never forget it.

Passive: The rope was thrown by the writer.

Active: The writer threw the rope.

For Strong Bones, Drink Your ... Beer?

Can beer really build strong bones? According to Tufts University's Katherine Tucker, associate professor of nutrition science and policy, beer contains a high level of silicon, which facilitates the deposit of calcium and other minerals into bones (Tufts E-News). Tucker says the benefit is there whether you drink light or dark beer, but that people should follow the consumption guidelines recommended by most experts-two drinks per day for men, and one for women.

Growth Management STRATEGIES

BETTER BUSINESS PERFORMANCE THROUGH PLANNING, STAFFING, TRAINING AND HUMAN RESOURCES–RELATED PROGRAMS   3RD QTR 2007

SPECIAL REPORT: Strategies for Retaining Your Top Talent

With the growing economy and low unemployment, it's a seller's market for job seekers. But as companies scramble to retain top talent, research shows that high salaries and perks simply aren't enough.

"Individuals with core competencies are in high demand, and many key technical people, are constantly looking for ways to learn and grow in their fields," says Bill Macaleer, founding partner of Growth Management Strategies (GMS). "Retention starts with providing these employees with the right kind of job – a position that presents ongoing opportunities for career growth."

Mentoring is one tool that many companies use successfully to provide staff with ongoing career development. An old concept with a new twist, today's mentoring programs are career-path development tools based on fostering relationships between experienced professionals and ambitious newcomers. Mentoring programs aren't just for new employees wanting to learn the ropes.

"Often in organizations you have seasoned, skilled employees who want to progress, but don't have the organizational savvy to do so," explains Macaleer. "You match these individuals with mentors who can teach them how to navigate and network to identify new career opportunities within the organization." High-potential staff can benefit from mentoring at any stage of their careers – even at the executive level. "We've found that even senior executives can use someone as their sounding board and confidant," says Macaleer.

The most important part of a mentoring program can also be the most difficult – accurately matching experience and skill sets of the mentors

continued on page 3 ... see Retaining Top Talent

Employee Communication: The Key to Surviving Corporate Change

Today, many businesses equate growth with success. Corporate mergers, acquisitions and restructuring are frequent and significant events in all sectors of the economy. But these changes, usually undertaken to raise profits and productivity, often bring unplanned side effects like increased turnover, productivity loss and lower morale.

A well-planned communication strategy launched early in any change event is one of the most successful ways to minimize disruption and retain key employees. It may seem obvious that

> "A well-planned communication strategy launched early in any change event is one of the most successful ways to minimize disruption and retain key employees."

people who believe they are being kept informed and are being treated fairly will be more committed to making the new organization a success. Yet most companies only give lip service to the importance of frequent, consistent communication with employees during transition times.

A good way to start informing employees of transition news is through existing communication channels: regular updates in employee publications, information on the company intranet, and in other employee communication vehicles. Other strategies may include management – employee small-group meetings and question and answer sessions with large groups. Providing an avenue for

continued on page 3 ... see Employee Communication

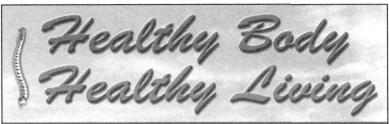

INFORMATION DEDICATED TO IMPROVING YOUR HEALTH AND WELLNESS THROUGH CHIROPRACTIC   VOLUME 6   ISSUE 10

H ello your customer's name!

Your name prints here is pleased to send you this issue of *Healthy Body Healthy Living*.

(Your personal message goes here)

Dear Doctor,

You are receiving this newsletter because you understand the importance of frequent contact with your patients. After all, your current patients hold the best prospects for future growth. This *Healthy Body Healthy Living* newsletter is part of an exciting new "Done for You – No Hassle" newsletter program that enables you to mail a full-color patient newsletter when you want, as often as you want, and quantity you want. These highly effective newsletters are written, designed, printed, and customized (with your name, contact information and your own personal message to your patients) for only 99 cents each! Plus, you can attach your mailing list and we will mail your newsletters for only 10 cents per newsletter! That's right – Dynamic Communication will address your newsletters, apply the postage, and deliver them to the post office – all for only 10 cents each! To learn more, and to save $199, please visit our Web site at www.dynamiccommunication.net.

Back Pain – Chiropractic Advice for Moms-to-Be

A s many new mothers can attest, the muscle strains of pregnancy are very real and can be more than just a nuisance. Studies have found that about half of all expectant mothers will develop low-back pain at some point during their pregnancies. During pregnancy, a woman's center of gravity almost immediately begins to shift forward to the front of her pelvis. As the baby grows, the woman's weight is projected even farther forward, and the curvature of her lower back is increased, placing extra stress on the spinal disks. In compensation, the normal curvature of the upper spine increases as well. While these changes sound dramatic, pregnancy hormones help loosen the ligaments attached to the pelvic bones. But even these natural changes designed to accommodate the growing baby can result in postural imbalances, making pregnant women prone to trips and falls.

How Can Your Doctor of Chiropractic Help?

Before you become pregnant, your doctor of chiropractic can detect any imbalances in your pelvis or elsewhere in your body that could contribute to discomfort during pregnancy or possible neuromusculoskeletal problems after childbirth.

Many pregnant women have found that chiropractic adjustments provide relief from the increased low-back pain brought on by pregnancy. Chiropractic manipulation is safe for the pregnant woman and her baby and can be especially attractive to those who are trying to avoid taking medications to treat their back pain. Doctors of chiropractic can also offer nutrition, ergonomic, and exercise advice to help a woman enjoy a healthy pregnancy.

Pregnancy Ergonomics: Your Bed and Desk

Sleep on your side with a pillow between your knees to take pressure off your lower back. Full-length "body pillows" or "pregnancy wedges" may be helpful. Lying on your left side allows unobstructed blood flow and assists kidney function.

Chiropractic care can also help after childbirth. In the eight weeks following delivery, the ligaments that loosened during pregnancy begin to tighten up again. Ideally, joint problems brought on during pregnancy from improper lifting or reaching should be treated before the ligaments return to their prepregnancy state. This will help prevent muscle tension, headaches, rib discomfort, and shoulder problems. - Adapted from the American Chiropractic Association www.acatoday.org

A NEWSLETTER OF FUN FACTS AND USEFUL INFORMATION FOR HOME OWNERS   VOL. 6 ISSUE 13

Hello Customer's Name!

This sample issue of *Your Home Address* has been sent to you courtesy of Your Name Here and the newsletter professionals at

(Your Logo here!)

Realtor News

If you made a down payment of less than 20 percent when you bought your home, you had to buy private mortgage insurance (PMI). The extra monthly charge of $50 to $100 for every $100,000 borrowed protects the lender against default. The problem is that PMI gets very expensive when you consider that it could take years to reach the 20 percent threshold where it is no longer required. The good news is that real estate in most areas has gone up in value. That means the equity you have in your home is much more than the amount you have paid off on your mortgage. It could have reached 20 percent or more.

Funny Bone

Quote on Willingness

The world is full of willing people. Some willing to work, the rest willing to let them.
— Robert Frost

To Sell Your House, Add Safety Features and Enhance Curb Appeal

First impressions are a powerful influence on home buyers. They can determine whether buyers fall in love with the idea of your house, and whether they want to look inside or just leave as quickly as possible. It doesn't take much to turn a prospect away. Unkempt grounds are a turnoff.

Leaves, unshoveled snow or uncut grass can cost you a sale. Real estate agents suggest walking up to your place to see if there is anything that looks unattractive or out of place.

Sprucing up the front yard is especially important. Planting flowers and shrubs costs some time and money, but can make the difference between a quick sale and one that takes much longer. Always plant flowers that complement the color of your home. Check the trim and repaint it if necessary. Make sure the gutters are clean. Many buyers today are concerned about safety. That's especially true of the one-third of all buyers who are single or single parents. Single women are a fast-growing segment of the market, real estate experts say. Along with the number of bedrooms and the square footage of the house, one single buyer specified an attached garage, a wall around the yard and neighbors. Other safety pluses include

- A security system
- Peepholes in exterior doors
- Lights in the yard and along patios and sidewalks
- A front door and windows that can be seen from the street and not hidden by tall bushes

If you are seeking a home and safety is a priority for you, avoid houses near shopping centers, malls or convenience stores that are open late. Don't buy a home on a busy street, next to a swimming pool or next to an apartment complex that is several stories high, say consultants writing in the Indianapolis Star.

Why Customer Newsletters Work So Darn Well

Next to a personal visit, nothing does more for building business than your own personalized newsletter. A professionally written, designed, and printed newsletter can be one of the most effective marketing weapons you have. Dollar for dollar, newsletters are the most effective marketing tool available. In addition to being a practical and affordable way to keep the vital communication link with your customers, a company newsletter can help grow your business. Here's how they work:

- Newsletters help you retain your customer base, increasing future business
- Stimulated by the reminder, customers are likely to refer friends and neighbors to you
- Most customers will share their newsletter, giving you extra free exposure!
- Stand apart – newsletters will help Differentiate you from your competitors
- Newsletters are an effective way to introduce new products or services

SAVE $99 NOW! Visit www.dynamiccommunication.net and create your on-line newsletter within 14 days of receiving this newsletter, and the $99 set up fee will be waived!!

INFORMATION ASSURANCE

NEWS AND INFORMATION DEDICATED TO THE AWARENESS AND ADVANCEMENT OF INFORMATION ASSURANCE EDUCATION   1ST QTR – 2007

Director's Notes ...

by Denise E. Spanish

I'd like to wish everyone a happy and healthy new year! We are finalizing the 2007 agenda for our continuing series of workshops and seminars. Our first event, a seminar in our Lunch Byte series, is on March 6. Details can be found on this page. We'll also soon be announcing more partnerships with historically black colleges and universities (HBCUs).

With the threats to our information security on the rise, it is important that everyone in your organization think like a chief security officer (CSO). CSOs make decisions with the interests and needs of their company in mind. A CSO has to know as much as possible about the business in order to establish reasonable protection priorities. No one can set security and risk priorities without understanding the business first. While the CSO has authority over the entire security function, an organization's security is greatly enhanced when everyone is aware of the various elements of security, particularly the human aspect, which is just as important as the technical.

This newsletter, as well as future issues, will explore in depth the human aspect of information assurance. Since the topic for my dissertation, which I am currently writing, is on social engineering, I am pleased to have Ira S. Winkler contribute an enlightening article on this subject. Winkler is recognized as one of the world's experts in Internet security, information warfare, information-related crime investigation, and industrial espionage. He is a specialist in penetration testing, where he infiltrates companies, both technically and physically, to find and repair an organization's weaknesses. His article appears on page two of this newsletter.

West Chester University Receives NSTISSI 4013 Renewal

West Chester University recently received a five-year renewal of the National Information Assurance Training Standard for System Administrators (NSTISSI) 4013 designation. The five-year redesignation is a prerequisite requirement for the National Centers of Academic Excellence in Information Assurance Education (CAEIAE). The Information Courseware Evaluation (IACE) Program is a major step in meeting the national requirements for information

Pictured from left: Dr. Linton Wells II, Ms. Denise Spanish, Mr. Rich Epstein, Dr. Dick Schaeffer, Ms. Nancy DeFrancesco, and Mr. Eustace King

assurance education and training. The award will be officially presented at the upcoming 11th annual Colloquium, which will take place at Boston University, Boston, Mass., June 4-7, 2007.

IAC Lunch Bytes

SECURING MOBILE/LAPTOP COMPUTING

Michael Piscopo has over 14 years in information technology, including security architecture and design, network engineering, real-time distributed computing, and application development. He is currently the president and CTO of PeriNet Technologies, an IT security and infrastructure company based in Newtown, Pa. Topics covered will include

- Latest threats/compromises
- Overview of a "secured" network
- Steps to a safer mobile environment and mitigating risk

When: Tuesday, March 6, 2007 – Noon to 1:00 p.m.
Where: Graduate Business Center – Greenhill Corporate Center
Cost: Free – Lunch will be provided!
Register: www.iacwcu.com
For More Information: 610-425-5000, ext. 2788

SUNSET *THE 800-LB GORILLA*

BRIDGE LOANS — CONVENTIONAL LOANS — PROBLEM LOAN SOLUTIONS

NEWS AND INFORMATION ABOUT COMMERCIAL LOANS AND BUSINESS DEVELOPMENT STRATEGIES   NOV/DEC 2005

On the Fast Track

SUNSET BRANCH EMPLOYEES EARN LARGE COMMISSIONS FOR REFERRALS

Welcome to the premier edition of *The 800-Lb Gorilla.* As you learned at Sunset's 2005 National Convention, the commercial loan division is enjoying great success in closing commercial loans. In addition to closing loans (see "Tombstones" on page 2), the referral program is beginning to pay big dividends for our Sunset branch employees. *The 800-Lb Gorilla* recently interviewed Steve Forman, vice president of Sunset Commercial Group, LLC.

Gorilla: First of all, what is "new" about the commercial loan division?
Steve: When I came on board, I quickly assessed the need to be more in touch with our network of Sunset branches. I believe "win-win" scenarios are the most effective ways to expand a business.

Steve Forman

Gorilla: What have you done to support the growth you're seeing, and to ensure that the loan approval process is a "win-win" for everyone involved?
Steve: We recognize that when a Sunset branch employee makes a referral, both the employee and the client want to get an answer as quickly as possible. To aid that effort, I hired Paul Scherbner, who has 23 years of experience in banking and was a former VP in a commercial loan department, to streamline the paperwork. Through Paul's leadership, the Sunset Commercial Group prepares a comprehensive 15-50 page credit write-up. We can often get a preliminary response in 24 hours. In addition, I believe that effective communication

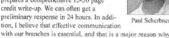
Paul Scherbner

with our branches is essential, and that is a major reason why we are proud to introduce our new 800-Lb Gorilla newsletter.

Gorilla: What is your goal for the commercial division?
Steve: Our goal is to rapidly expand the opportunities for Sunset branch employees to offer commercial loan services and to increase their income potential.

Marketing Tip

THE MOST IMPORTANT MARKETING TOOL YOU HAVE

What's the most important marketing tool you have? A few hints: It's small, it's inexpensive, and you probably don't consider it as part of your marketing plan.

It's your business card!

Many people think of their business card as just a reference document, a way to tell someone your address and phone number. By looking at your business card as a marketing tool, you can open up a new way of thinking about that small but powerful piece of cardstock.

At a minimum, does your business card convey exactly what you do? Does your business card list "residential mortgage specialist" and does it mention that you offer commercial loans? Perhaps you might want to have different business cards for different purposes.

Take a fresh look at your business card. Does it help people remember you? Does it motivate them to do business with you? At the very least, is the information clear? Are you one of those people who never seems to have a business card on hand? If so, then you will want to break the habit of forgetting to bring your cards along.

Not having your business card on you is a social faux pas. When someone asks you for a card, he or she is complimenting you. It means the person likes you and might be willing to do business with you in the future. Not having the card with you is embarrassing for both of you. It also puts your reputation on the line. After all, what kind of a business person doesn't have a card on hand? It communicates that you might not be serious about your job, your business, or your life – and that you can't be trusted with the other person's business.

SUNSET COMMERCIAL GROUP, LLC   ●   THREE DICKENSON DRIVE – CHADDS FORD, PA 19317   ●   888-378-6736

Jesus is the Way
OUTREACH MINISTRIES

PROMOTING FAITH, UNITY, AND SALVATION

A Personal Mission to Encourage Faith and Community

The Story of Jesus is the Way Outreach Ministries
by Dr. Kara Conliffe

I was raised in the suburbs of Bloomfield Hills, Michigan, and attended Michigan State University. After graduating from Meharry Medical College, I received my medical degree and completed my residency in anesthesiology at Northwestern University in Chicago. I met my husband, Ted, while at school and we now have four beautiful children.

I always make a point of praying silently for my patients. One day at the hospital, I began noticing many patients around the hospital wearing wristbands with various sayings. One day the Holy Spirit put on my heart ad idea that would help others have a relationship with Jesus Christ and easily identify fellow believers, therefore encouraging community. The idea was design a wristband with the words, "Jesus is the Way." This would be both a visible sign to fellow believers, and serve as a conversation starter to those that are not yet saved. So, in 2005, I established Jesus is the Way Outreach Ministries.

The wristbands have worked so well that Jesus is the Way has added an apparel line which includes tote bags, t-shirts, caps and sling packs that carry the Jesus is the Way logo, serving as a reminder to grow spiritually and emotionally in order to positively impact local communities. I am now working to expand the ministry by exploring ways to work with churches and other ministries on various fund-raising events, offering Jesus is the Way merchandise at a discount. To help us reach our young adults, we are also printing our caps in the colors of our schools and universities. The good Lord asks us to be bold and share the gospel with others. If you would like to find out more, please visit www.jesusistheway.biz.

For Your Next Fundraiser, Partner With Jesus is the Way!

"All things are possible to him who believes."
Mark 9:14-23

The ministry that started with the phrase *Jesus is the Way* imprinted on a simple purple wristband has developed into a growing movement with national and international goals. "While our logo appears on many different items, it is not about the item, it is about the message,"says Jesus is the Way founder, Dr. Kara Conliffe. "There is no limit to the number of items that we can apply the logo to and we will work with ministires or companies to discuss the best way to spread the word" Dr. Conliffe continued.

Jesus is the Way outreach ministry products are the perfect vehicle for many Christian-based fundraisers. Jesus is the Way is currently seeking to partner with churches, outreach organizations, and other ministries that share the same goal of introducing non-believers to the awesome power and glory of Jesus Christ. Jesus is the Way is pleased to extend a 20% discount to groups and organizations purchasing their products in quantity. For large organizations, additional discount programs are available. Dr. Kara would like to hear from your group or organization on how we can partner together. "God has put on my heart to start this ministry because so many people are not saved, and don't know that Jesus is the Way. It is my hope that our products will simply get a conversation started by having someone ask, Jesus is the Way to what? I look forward to hearing from you soon." This unique ministry has a very simple goal. They would like to see the Christians around the globe wearing the wristbands. The wristbands make it easy for believers to "wear their faith on their sleeve"and identify themselves to other brothers and sisters in Christ.

> "God has put on my heart to start this ministry because so many people are not saved, and don't know that Jesus is the Way.

JESUS IS THE WAY OUTREACH MINISTRIES ● P.O. BOX 4651 – CHERRY HILL, NJ 08034 ● 856-220-4954 ● WWW.JESUSISTHEWAY.BIZ

Security Cubed

VIP CLIENT NEWSLETTER

A MONTHLY CLIENT NEWSLETTER FROM THE RESIDENTIAL AND COMMERCIAL SECURITY EXPERTS AT SECURITY CUBED   MAY 2007

Hello [customer name]!

This newsletter is sent to you courtesy of the security pros at

It is our way of saying that you are important to us and we truly value your business. Please feel free to pass this newsletter on to friends and neighbors. Enjoy!

Funny Bone

Five Things My Mother Taught Me

1. My mother taught me about ANTICIPATION ... "Just wait until your father gets home."

2. My mother taught me about RECEIVING .... "You are going to get it when we get home!"

3. My mother taught me to MEET A CHALLENGE ... "What were you thinking? Answer me when I talk to you! Don't talk back to me!"

4. My mother taught me LOGIC ... "If you fall out off that swing and break your neck, you're not going to the store with me."

5. My mother taught me MEDICAL SCIENCE ... "If you don't stop crossing your eyes, they are going to freeze that way."

Learning to Take Advice Can Make All the Difference

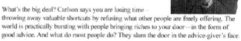

Many people in our lives are willing to help us, says *Don't Worry, Make Money* author Richard Carlson. The problem is, he says, that most people are completely unwilling to take another person's advice—no matter how sincerely helpful and competent the advice giver is. Carlson says that most people suffer from stubbornness and don't listen to others—and absolutely refuse to take advice.

What's the big deal? Carlson says you are losing time — throwing away valuable shortcuts by refusing what other people are freely offering. The world is practically bursting with people bringing riches to your door—in the form of good advice. And what do most people do? They slam the door in the advice-giver's face.

Carlson says you should do yourself a favor and show some humility. The next time someone gives you a piece of advice and your impulse is not to take it stop and consider whether the advice is what you need or not. If the advice is good, make sure you tell the person who is giving it to you that you think it's great. Make the other person happy in the process of taking the advice. You'll be glad you did.

First, Do No Harm

If you have an employee you feel needs to be reprimanded or even demoted or fired, make sure you question yourself about how the situation has come about. Before you take any action, ask yourself whether your standards are reasonable. You shouldn't tolerate shoddy work, but you also need to ask yourself where you are on the work-quality scale. Do people always seem to fail to meet your standards? Are there only a couple of people (and one of them is you!) who ever seems to consistently do a good job? Do your standards fit the job you are doing? Are you constantly redoing your workers' work because you think they are not meeting the mark? If so, the problem could be that your standards are too high and have become obstacles to those you are in charge of-and keep them from getting their work done. This is a painful problem for managers to cop to-after all, no one wants to lower his or her standards in the workplace. Having high standards is probably what got you where you are in the first place. But if you are always second-guessing your workers' work and double-checking every project before you let it go out the door, it's likely that you have a problem with letting things go – and letting others take responsibility for their work.

Mauger & Company's

HOME COMFORT

Mauger & Company's news and information about heating, cooling, and maintaining your home   Spring 2007

The Ever-Changing Prices of Heating Oil

Hello and happy spring to all of our loyal customers. Even in the heating oil business, we're happy to see the warm weather! Heating oil pricing for the upcoming 2007/08 heating season has been the main topic around our offices for the last few weeks, so I've asked our controller, Steve Schramm, if he would write our lead article for this issue of *Home Comfort*. I wish you all a wonderful summer!

Bud Mauger, President
bmauger@maugerco.com

Fixed Price versus Market Price?
By Stephen Schramm, Controller

When buying your heating oil, which option is better for you? First and foremost, by signing a fixed-price contract, you are not guaranteed the best or lowest price of oil for a heating season. In fact, during the last heating season market pricing ran 20 cents or more below our fixed price. In my twelve years of experience with fixed prices, this is only the third time this has happened. That's a ratio of 4 to 1 in favor of fixed prices. However, the real reason the fixed-price concept came about was to stabilize the cost of oil over a given heating season, eliminating the peaks and valleys that can occur over a nine-month period. The second reason is to help you budget your cost for the season.

An oil marketer's life would be less complicated if we sold our oil using only market pricing. What's the right price? What quantity of oil do we need to price protect with our suppliers? What's the temperature going to be this season? Why do we use a written agreement? Can and how do we allow an exit from the contract? You need a crystal ball to make all the choices. All these questions go away when you sell strictly by market price

Let's address some of these questions and others that are frequently asked by our customers. Why a written agreement? The answer is easy; for both your protection and ours. It is our opinion that any reputable company should be willing to put their commitment in writing. Why does the customer choose the gallons to price protect? There is no way we can anticipate all our customers needs. Your circumstances

continued on page 3 ... heating oil

The Importance of Safety
By George Mezzachio

In the fuel delivery business, "better safe than sorry", is not just a cliché, it is a way of life. Every day, our drivers are put to the task. They are responsible for the safe delivery of product to our customers while negotiating tricky road conditions, vehicle maintenance, weight and height restrictions, traffic, as well as the conditions that exist at each delivery site. Their diligence is necessary in order for them to maintain their D.O.T. commercial license and therefore their ability to make a living. We at Mauger value our drivers and would like to take this opportunity to recognize

- Jerry Baugher
- Joe Gallagher
- Harry Powell
- Bob Erickson
- Dan Clifford
- Pat Ferrara
- John Blair
- Ken Dejewski
- Mike Gledhill
- Wilson Acevido
- Jeff Schell
- Antonio Fuentes
- Steve Henthorn
- Ron Smith

Without these individuals we could not go about doing the business of getting product to you on time and safely.

The Dangers of Carbon Monoxide

Many people are not aware that Carbon monoxide can exist in their homes and what sources might produce this odorless and colorless gas. Without a proper detection device, many people may never know that they have been exposed. Some of the ways that carbon monoxide can be produced include cars running in a closed attached garage, improperly vented heating equipment and stoves, gas logs or natural wood burning fireplaces, gas grills and gas dryers. Mauger and Company strongly suggests that if you install a carbon monoxide detector to protect the health of you and your family.

Your Name Prints Here **presents**

MAGICAL HAPPENINGS

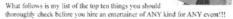

A MAGICAL "GOOD NEWS" NEWSLETTER FULL OF FUN INFORMATION FOR OUR CUSTOMERS   APRIL 2008

A Magical Hello to You!

This issue of *Magical Success* is being sent to you courtesy of

two lines available for company name and/or sender's name

It is our way of saying that you are important to us and we truly value your business. Please feel free to pass this newsletter on to friends and neighbors. Enjoy!

A Few Words from Our Customers ....

text box for customer testimonials

There is room for approximately 120 words or 750 characters

SPECIAL REPORT... The Top Ten Biggest Mistakes Event Planners Make When Booking Entertainment and How to Avoid Them!

Booking entertainment for your event can be a daunting task! You want it to be fun for everyone, extra special and stay within your budget. Where do you start? What can you do to ensure a successful event? How do you know you are making the right choice?

Questions like these prompted me to write this report. Having been in the entertainment industry for many years, I have seen event planners make MAJOR mistakes that could have very easily been avoided if they had asked a few simple questions up front – BEFORE the day of the event!

What follows is my list of the top ten things you should thoroughly check before you hire an entertainer of ANY kind for ANY event!!!

1) Begin with someone you have already seen or someone who has been recommended to you. This is your number one resource by far! If you haven't personally seen an entertainer who meets your needs, ask your friends, colleagues and family. It is much better to get someone you can trust right from the start.

2) Ask for references and call them! If the performer wasn't personally recommended to you, by all means do your research! Ask for references. If the performer can't provide you with some or has some excuse for not giving out names or something ridiculous like that, DO NOT engage this entertainer.

I know of an entertainer in my area who works a lot. He does quite a few shows, but never at the same place twice! RED FLAG!!! He's a great marketer/salesman, but it ends there. Call the references and ask some questions.

3) The next step beyond references is experience. Think of yourself as a Human Resource Director. After all, you are considering hiring this person, even if for a short time. Where has he or she performed before? What awards or accolades has this person received? Is he a beginner or a seasoned professional?

4) Is the performer's act age appropriate? This is a question that rarely gets asked but is supremely important! Is the entertainer used to working with your type of audience? Example: He/She may be a wonderful magician and may have done a great job at little Johnny's 4th Birthday Party, but this material will not work for your corporate clients. And visa-versa, let's say he is a great sleight-of-hand artist, but if he doesn't have any experience entertaining children, they will eat him alive!

I'll be back next month with the rest of this insightful report! See you then!

PA CHIROPRACTIC ASSOCIATION

Promoting the Highest Level of Quality Chiropractic Care Through Integrity, Access and Education

July Convention 2007 "This Year We Go Over the Top!"

You have asked for more and we have complied! This year's convention will be one of the most diverse conventions to date. Here are just a few of the highlights that await you at Seven Springs Mountain Resort from July 19 - 22, 2007:

Education

- 8 CE hours on Thursday - Rehabilitation and Philosophy
  - Bryanne Enterprises sponsoring Dr. Jay Kennedy - 6 CE hours on "AFM, DTS, Laser and Rehabilitation"
  - TLC for Superteams sponsoring Dr. Dean DePice - 2 CE hours on "Recognizing Challenges Within the Profession & Validating Chiropractic"
- PCA New Doctor Program on Thursday
  - Focus on responsibilities, management and coding issues
- 14 hours CE on Saturday and Sunday - "Evidenced Based Approach to Lumbar Spine"
  - NCMIC sponsoring Dr. Mike Schneider - 6 CE hours Saturday and 8
- CA Training all day Saturday
  - Sponsored by Integrity Management with Ms. Cheri Gage
- CPR offered at an additional cost Sunday morning - re-certifications only

Golf

- Convention's golf extravaganza - "The Hubie" will once again be offered to the winning team - additional cost for greens fees, cart and lunch
- 1:00 PM Shotgun Thursday at Seven Springs Mountain Course

Management

Friday - full day of Practice Management!
- Breakthrough Coaching - Dr. Jeff Lewin
  - "Can your Practice Survive a Post Payment Audit?"
- Integrity Management - Dr. David Kats
  - "How to Grow a 50% Maintenance Practice"

- TLC for Superteams - Dr. Dean DePice
  - "Practice, Promote and Prosper" & "Attrack, Provide & Collect More"
- Individual break-out sessions with exhibitors and vendors

Business

- PCA Board of Director's Meeting on Friday morning
- PCA Annual Business Meeting/Breakfast on Saturday
- PCA Annual Business on Saturday morning
- Re-Organizational Board Meeting on Sunday morning

Social Events

- Thursday Luncheon provided by Brican - sponsoring Stanley B. Greenfield - RHU presenting:
  - "Are You Getting Your Money's Worth?"

(continued on page 4 ... see Convention 2007)

IN THIS ISSUE

143

Novello's

Personal Style

Information and tips on hair, skin, nails, and looking & feeling great!   3rd Quarter – 2003

Finding the Hair Style That Suits You

While we all have individual hair preferences, there are a few rules of thumb – based on the shape and features of your face, the texture of your hair, your age and your lifestyle – that can help you find and keep your best, most wearable style.

Face shape and features

The shape of your face and the proportions of your features will help tell you what hairstyle is perfect for you:

• Oval-shaped face: Lucky you! You have the kind of face shape that lets you wear your hair just about any way you choose. The forehead and chin of an oval face are in proportion to each another, making both long and short cuts look great on you.

• Round face: To get the illusion of a narrower face, try a cut with layers and fullness on top, but keep it close to your face at the sides. Go either short or longer than chin length, swept back from your forehead, with wispy fringes or parted on the side. A rounded style that ends at your chin will emphasize the shape of your face.

• Heart-shaped face: Those with a heart-shaped face know that the jaw and forehead often look wide, and the chin can appear pointy. Short hair usually works well for this face shape; a thick, chopped, layered cut or a pixie cut is a good choice because the hair is full on top, evening out the jaw and chin lines.

• Full forehead, long chin: If you have a full forehead and a long chin, it helps to add volume below the chin to balance things out a bit. A medium-length bob or a thick, layered cut lends fullness where it's needed. Fringes can also help reduce the appearance of a large forehead.

• Large features: If you're supersensitive about the size of your nose or any other part of your face, you can de-emphasize these features with fullness in the hair. Straight hair parted in the middle makes a prominent nose seem even more so – as does a long, heavy fringe – but a fuller style takes the emphasis off and balances out large features. Soft, subtle highlights can also help by drawing the eye away from the face and toward the hair.

Making Your Manicure Last

Ever had a manicure that you're wild about when you leave the salon, only to find that it's chipping by dinnertime? Try these easy tips to maintain glam hands:

1. Start well. Make sure you have clean nails before applying varnish. If you have hand lotion or a build-up of natural oils on your nails, it will cause the polish to peel. Swab the nails first with a nail varnish remover. Then, wash nails with soap and water.

2. Don't cut corners. After filing nails to their desired length, use a base coat, apply the varnish, then finish with a top coat. It's sometimes tempting to skip the base and top coat if you're in a hurry, but it's not worth doing this because it could make your varnish chip straightaway.

3. Be patient. Let each coat dry for a couple of minutes before applying another. This allows the polish to set so the next layer adheres better. Try to avoid using fast-drying varnishes because they don't last as long as regular ones.

4. Be precious. Always treat your nails as if you've just had them polished. Wear gloves whenever you do daily manual tasks, such as cleaning or gardening.

5. Be careful. Try not to use your nails as tools. Concentrate on using the pads of your fingers and not your fingertips when you reach, grab, hold and type.

Meet the Stylists

In this issue of *Personal Style,* we're pleased to introduce **Kim Merchenthaler.** Kim is a licensed cosmetology teacher and specializes in color and cuts. Kim was schooled at Gordon Phillips and has over 10 years' experience. When not pleasing customers, Kim enjoys spending time with her 4-year old son.

BUSINESS DEVELOPMENT SOLUTIONS THAT CONTRIBUTE TO GROWTH AND PRODUCTIVITY WHILE ALWAYS AIMING AT EXCELLENCE — VOL. 6, NO. 1

The Premier Edition of *On-Target Business Solutions*!

Welcome to the premier edition of *On-Target Business Solutions*. Produced by ABC Consulting Group International, LLC (ABC), this newsletter is designed to provide information about business development solutions that can contribute to your company's growth and productivity. In this first issue, we're pleased to interview Franck J. Gerard, the founder and CEO of ABC Consulting Group.

How does ABC define success?
We define success as adding value to the lives of professionals and always aiming at excellence. We have learned that most successful organizations have one thing in common: They're eager to invest in the development of their people by equipping them with the knowledge, skills and leadership necessary for corporate success.

How would you describe your business model?
ABC consistently achieves tangible results for clients using our proprietary A³ Excellence™ Business Model. Our business model is successful because we evaluate, educate and motivate our client's team to produce significant and consistent results. We've successfully completed instructional design projects, business development initiatives and leadership coaching sessions using the guidelines of our business model.

What are ABC's core programs?
Our Project Management series, including our very successful 3² Project Management™ Certificate Track, as well as our Leadership for the Project Manager and our Project Cost Management seminars, offer a great combination of technical and people skills, and tools and principles that everyone can readily and successfully apply to their everyday responsibilities.

What other training programs does your company offer?
ABC is certified by Maximum Impact, the company founded by New York Times best-selling author Dr. John C. Maxwell, to present the seminar Developing The Leader Within You®. We also frequently speak at Temple University's Fox School of Business on strategic thinking, leadership and time management, as well as offer our one-day courses, I™ Thinking Forward, Called to Leadership and, one of my favorites, Time Waits For No One.

Who is your time management program designed for?
If you've ever said, "I'm just so busy" or "I'm always running out of time," this program is for you. We teach people how to take control of their day and week by learning to prioritize effectively, understanding the value of time and learning to invest time, not just spend it!

When are your training programs offered?
The best way to find more information about our programs and services is to visit our Web site at **www.abc-advantage.com**.

The 3² Project Management™ METHODOLOGY

Add "project manager" to your professional profile

Imagine achieving your objectives, meeting your deadlines, controlling your budget and managing your role as a project leader or project team member. This PMI®-designated certificate program is the foundation on which project management expertise is built.

The workshop consists of three powerful sessions as outlined below:

Back to Square One
Although often neglected, the highly critical project conceptualization phase sets the stage for success. During this phase, a project manager and team will establish a project's value and communicate its scope by answering the what, why, how and how much of each project.

Planning for Success
The planning stage of any project is crucial to its on-going progress and successful completion. Skip it at your own risk! Place your important project(s) "under the microscope" and perform a careful analysis of task order (who is doing what and when) so that — as a project manager — you can efficiently organize work flow, carefully assign resources, describe work assignments and precisely schedule resources and deliverables.

The Measure of Success
As a project manager, you'll find yourself clarifying expectations, shuffling resources, changing targets, negotiating support, analyzing reports, adjusting budgets, sharing options (rather than problems) and communicating constantly. A well-planned project execution phase will allow you to prevent "scope creep," manage the unexpected, and keep your team on track.

To attend this dynamic workshop, please visit the On-Target Learning Web site at **www.on-targetlearning.com**.

 Project Management Institute

ON♦TARGET is a publication of ABC Consulting Group Int'l, LLC • P.O. Box 337 • Willingboro, NJ 08046 • 609-880-0697 • www.on-targetlearning.com

LEADERSHIP FOCUS

PROFESSIONAL SERVICES   News and Information about Delivering Excellence in Managed Services   2nd Quarter – 2007

Building a President's Award Leader: Sandy Melnikoff

REGIONAL OPERATIONS MANAGER SANDY MELNIKOFF was awestruck when she heard Ira Levy, President and CEO, announce at this year's Annual Meeting that she was the recipient of the President's Award. In her acceptance speech, Sandy, the first woman to win the award, turned to her managers and said, "Thanks for making me look this good!"

Sandy receiving the President's Award from Ira Levy

This statement gives us great insight into Sandy's formula for success. "I don't care what business you are in, nobody is successful all by themselves," Sandy exclaimed. "It is a humbling experience, to sit at a table with the great leaders from my region all around me. How do I go up there to be recognized without recognizing them?"

Sandy credits Professional Services for the strength of her team. "Professional Services provides the best training and surrounds us with the best people. My job is to give them the support and tools to be successful. Developing them to their fullest potential requires the ability to be demanding and empower them at the same time."

Another important element of Sandy's success is the entrepreneurial style Professional Services employs. "Within the framework that Senior Management sets for us and with their guidance, I always manage my region as if it were my own company. I think like an entrepreneur, and they support me. I try to pass that on to my people with the agreement that everything they do must be high quality, within budget; and must demand the very best of themselves and their teams."

Sandy brought this attitude with her when she came to the company. Her mentor was her father, who was known as "Red" in the small town where she grew up in Pennsylvania. "Red" was the fire chief, a police officer, a truck driver, and known all over town. Her mother was the PTA President. "Mom and Dad developed my sense of independence; but they were careful to teach me that responsibility goes with it," said Sandy. "They also taught me that people and their families are important. I watched how they led those around them and saw what worked. First, they respected the people around them; second, they enabled people's independence with responsibility; and third, people gave that respect back tenfold."

Sandy also credits the Senior Management Team for her professional growth. "They are very supportive, in the same ways Dad was. They give me independence and responsibility, but they're there to make me successful. Beginning with Ira Levy, each one of the Senior Managers has helped me to grow," said Sandy. "Consequently, we all have accountability to Professional Services because the company is so committed to developing us as leaders. We cannot be satisfied doing just a good job; we have to be doing a great job and be recognized in our hospitals as leaders."

Sandy has successfully retained her accounts, renewed contracts, satisfied demanding clients, opened new business, and sold additional business. Yet, she maintains that her greatest achievement at Professional has been "Building my management team, person by person. Obviously, they make me look good."

Congratulations, Sandy, on being recognized with a President's Award.

2006 President's Award Recipient, Sandy Melnikoff

IN THIS ISSUE

146

CHRISTIAN CHAMBER OF COMMERCE

Living the Word

BRINGING BUSINESS PEOPLE TOGETHER TO ADVANCE THE KINGDOM OF GOD AND THEIR INDIVIDUAL ENTERPRISES FOR THE LORD JESUS CHRIST   2ND QTR 2009

Focusing on Others

Our gracious and loving God has placed on my heart to use this column to address the following question – *What can we do to help each other?*

Many of us struggle with the concept of giving. How much is enough and how can we give when we ourselves have so many pressing financial concerns? However, instead of focusing on money, I would like to talk about the other side of giving – the giving of ourselves. In 1 Peter 4:10 it reads, "Each one should use whatever gift he has received to serve others, faithfully administering God's grace in its various forms." In James 1:17 we read, "Every good gift and every perfect gift is from above, and comes down from the Father of lights."

The Chamber was blessed in a big way a few weeks ago when Steve Marr agreed to fly in from Arizona to speak to our members about building our businesses God's Way. When I asked Steve to speak to our chamber, he told me that he doesn't do anything without first praying about it. Steve called me a few days later and told me that God wanted him in New Jersey to speak to our group! What a great example of God's Grace! The Christian Chamber of Commerce has also been blessed with members from many different industries who are possessed of a variety of skills. From my perspective, the one characteristic that we all have in common is a desire and a willingness to help our brothers and sisters in Christ. It frequently occurs to me that this Chamber offers a wealth of opportunities for each of us to serve the Lord by reaching out and serving each other. I truly hope that happens.

God will bless us if we are generous. "Give, and it will be given to you; good measure, pressed down, shaken together, and running over will be put into your bosom. For with the same measure that you use, it will be measured back to you" (Luke 6:38). If we use a teaspoon to measure out our giving, God will use a teaspoon to measure out our blessings. If we use a dump truck to give, God will use a dump truck to bless us spiritually. I encourage all of you to come to our networking breakfasts and monthly luncheons. When you arrive, walk up to someone you don't know and, before exchanging business cards, extend your hand in friendship. Ask each person you meet, "How can I help you?" I know in my heart that God will smile on you and who knows, you might just be driving home in a dump truck!

In His service,

Angela Pipersburgh
President

Witnessing – Doing Business God's Way

Integrity - Make It Your Niche by Will Shelley

When I sat down to share a piece of myself with this great organization, I felt compelled to open my sword for a word that has been a speaking and working guide for my life.

In 1 Kings 9:3-5, the Lord said to Solomon, "I have heard the prayer and plea you have made before me: I have consecrated this temple, which you have built, by putting my Name there forever. My eyes and my heart will always be there. As for you, if you walk before me in integrity of heart and uprightness, as David your father did, and do all I command and observe my decrees and laws, I will establish your royal throne over Israel forever, as I promised David your father when I said, 'You shall never fail to have a man on the throne of Israel.'"

This particular scripture is what has made me understand that all things belong to God. In 2003, I asked my Lord and Savior what direction I should take my life and He placed a word on my heart - INTEGRITY. Throughout my career, I have worked for many different companies. No matter what the company, I never felt comfortable with the often referenced rule, "forget what the procedure is, this is how we do things here." The Word says, "As for you, if you walk before me in integrity of heart and uprightness ... " That means be sound and congruent in the things you do, follow the procedures and codes of conduct, and don't defraud the company or your customers.

God has made us just a little lower than the angels; He has given us dominion over many things. Instead of taking and looking for shortcuts, strive to be righteous. Since God has blessed me with the vision of being a business owner, I've often been asked, "What is your

niche; what makes W.E. Shelley & Associates different?" God promised me that He would never leave me or forsake me. That remains deeply imbedded in my mind. The difference for me is that holiness is right and if I live each day according to God's will, with integrity, His hedge of protection will be securely around me.

In Proverbs 10:9 it reads, "The man of integrity walks securely, but he who walks crooked paths will be found out." Living the word of the Lord is my niche, and I thank God for giving me this vision.

Your Company Name **presents**

March 2007

IN TOUCH

The **ULTIMATE** Customer Newsletter!

IN THIS ISSUE

When to Call Tech Support

If You Just Had Time!

Funny Bone

Be a Great Conversationalist

Hello!

This issue of *In Touch* is being sent to you courtesy of

two lines available for company name and/or sender's name

It is our way of saying that you are important to us and we truly value your business. Please feel free to pass this newsletter on to friends and neighbors. Enjoy!

Funny Bone

Best Excuses When Caught Sleeping at Your Desk

1. They told me at the blood bank that this might happen.

2. This is just a 15-minute power nap, like they raved about in the last time-management course you sent me to.

3. Whew! Guess I left the top off the Liquid Paper.

4. I wasn't sleeping! I was meditating on the mission statement and envisioning a new paradigm!

5. This is one of the seven habits of highly effective people.

6. I was testing the keyboard for drool resistance.

7. The coffee machine is broken.

8. Boy, that cold medicine I took last night just won't wear off.

From Ahajokes.com

Ask These Questions to Progress in Your Work Life

Are you unhappy with where you are in your work life? If you are, then you probably need to take stock of your life and where you want to be. To create movement in a desired direction in your life, the first thing you have to determine is where you want to go. What is your goal? Do you want to be a manager? Do you want to work in technology, but right now you're working in advertising? Assess what it is that will make you happier and more fulfilled - then figure out why you are not already doing it. Here's how:

• Ask yourself if you have any bad habits that are holding you back. If so, what are they? Can you eliminate them yourself or do you need help?

• Determine your strengths and whether you are using them to full advantage. If not, what do you need to do to activate them?

• Identify those on your support team. Do you have all the support you feel you need?

When You Call for Tech Support

If you have a personal computer and you call the 800 number for technical support, you should ask pointed questions about what you are being told. If an answer sounds fishy, you might be on to something. Ask to talk to a manager or someone who has experience with the exact problem you are seeking to solve. Or call back and work with another technician.

Workplace: Volunteering Is Good for Business, Good for You

A body of research shows that helping others can significantly reduce stress and enhance personal health. This helping requires personal contact with those helped, repetition at least every other week, and helping strangers rather than people you know. Such volunteers, scientists say, are focusing outside of themselves. Right now, only about 13 percent of Americans volunteer to help others face to face. Lack of time is the most common reason given. A survey by Big Brothers Big Sisters in New York, however, shows no difference in the amount of time spent on working or leisure between volunteers and nonvolunteers of similar backgrounds. A few people are self-starting volunteers, but most people say they considered volunteering for years before they did it. A survey by Spirituality & Health magazine shows that a majority of Americans would become person-contact volunteers if they could do it while at work. Others would do it if they received health insurance deductions.

NEWS AND INFORMATION FOR PROFESSIONAL ROOFING CONTRACTORS AND INSTALLERS EDITION **1** VOLUME **1**

Roofers News Debuts With Introduction to the Roofers Buggy

Welcome to the premier edition of *Roofers News*. This quarterly newsletter will present news and information designed to help roofing contractors and installers become more efficient and deliver better service to their customers.

In this premier issue, we're pleased to interview Aaron Beiler, the founder and president of Roofers Buggy, LLC.

Aaron Beiler

What prompted you to invent the Roofers Buggy?

I have owned and operated a roofing company for 18 years. As most roofers will agree, stripping old material from a house roof in order to put on a new roof is a time-consuming and dirty job. Often, the old material is thrown to the ground and then picked up manually. A common method of disposal is to move a truck near the building, but this is not always convenient or possible. I knew that there had to be a better way, so I invented the Roofers Buggy.

Roofers Buggy is towable

How does the Roofers Buggy work?

The Roofers Buggy is a self-propelled, towable unit that can lift, dump, and extend its 6-foot-by-8-foot container rearward while holding up to 4,000 pounds of debris or materials. The drive

Buggy is easy to drive on job site

system is easy to operate and gives you the ability to drive and maneuver the Buggy conveniently around the job site.

Roof clean off without the Roofers Buggy

When in place close to the roof, debris goes into the Buggy.

When it's in position close to the building, the container can be raised and its main beams extended out six and a half feet behind the rear wheelbase. This gives it the ability to place the container over shrubbery and under the roof edge. Shingle debris can then be pushed directly into the Buggy, keeping it off of the landscaping.

What do you do when the container is full?

When the container is full, it can be lifted (up to 11 feet) and dumped into a larger container, such as a dumpster or dump truck. Or, you can connect the Buggy to a vehicle and transport the debris to a landfill or dumping facility.

What are some of the features that are built into the Roofers Buggy?

The Roofers Buggy is very easy to operate. The

Buggy easily empties into truck

front-wheel system uses hydraulics to steer the Buggy. When the front wheels are lowered, the drive system is engaged, and when the front wheels are retracted, the drive system automatically disengages. The Buggy is also compact and needs only a six-foot opening to get through a privacy area or

continued on back page ... see Roofers Buggy

 *presents*

Comfort Solutions

Timothy Off's News and Information About Heating, Cooling, and Creating Comfort in Your Home   Fall 2007

Welcome to Comfort Solutions!

Hello and welcome to the premier issue of *Comfort Solutions*, our biannual customer newsletter. This newsletter is just one of the ways that we want to convey our appreciation and gratitude for your business. We hope that you enjoy reading it, and please feel free to pass it on to your friends and neighbors.

As we approach the fall and winter heating season, I want to discuss the benefits of adding a new humidifier to your heating system. Conditioning the amount of moisture in the air with a furnace humidifier is an important part of taking care of your family's health. Dry air in your home can make your throat feel dry and cause or aggravate respiratory ailments. Inadequate humidification during cold weather is one of the major causes of respiratory infections. Please call our office for a quote on installing a humidifier on your furnace.

If the humidifier on your furnace is 10 years old or older, I strongly encourage you to have one of our technicians inspect it. Since the water evacuation system on an older humidifier allows water to collect for a period of time, it is a perfect place for mold to develop.

I also want to mention that we have installed a new computer scheduling system that automatically prompts our staff to schedule your cleaning and service calls. Or, if you prefer, you can also schedule a service call by logging on to our Web site, **www.timothyoffheating.com**.

Timothy Off Heating and Air Conditioning offers a variety of service programs to ensure that your heating and air-conditioning systems are maintained and keep you comfortable all year round. You can see some of the options on the back page.

Timothy Off, President
info@timothyoffheating.com

Energy Efficiency Means Money Saved

Focus on protecting the environment and saving money. The more energy efficient we are at home and work, the more we save money, conserve energy resources, and protect the environment. It's especially important to be energy conscious during the winter, since much energy can be used up by inefficient appliances and poorly insulated homes. Here are a few more money-and energy-saving tips:

✓ **Cut your utility bill by 30 percent** by using appliances that have the Energy Star label. The label indicates that an appliance or home item is energy efficient.

✓ **Give your heating and cooling systems a tune-up.** Cooling and heating make up almost half of a family's energy bill. Make sure the filters are clean and the equipment is working properly so that it runs.

✓ **Unplug items that cause hidden energy leaks.** Many appliances that have display clocks and memory chips (like CD players and microwave ovens) consume energy even when they're turned off. These energy "leaks" cost Americans $3 billion annually.

✓ **Let the sun in.** Open curtains and blinds during the day to let the sun warm your home. Close them during the evening to conserve the heat.

✓ **Switch to fluorescent bulbs.** If you replaced the four most used 100-watt incandescent bulbs in your home with four comparable 23-watt fluorescent bulbs, you'd save $82 over three years. If all U.S. households replaced incandescent bulbs, the nation would save as much energy as the amount produced by 30 power plants annually.

The Risk Factor

NEWSLETTER

PEOPLE • PROCESSES • BUILDINGS • ENVIRONMENT

DEDICATED TO THE SAFETY AND HEALTH OF YOUR BUSINESS AND ITS EMPLOYEES   2ND QTR – 2006

Ergonomics: Micro to Macro Success Stories

The OSHA ergonomics standard was rescinded several years ago, yet many companies continue to establish and/or expand ergonomics programs in their workplaces. Why is that? The reason is that effective ergonomics programs save companies money!

Ergonomic risk factors in the workplace continue to plague many employers. In Pennsylvania in 2004, sprains and strains represented 43.1 percent of the claims by nature of injury. The number one cause of accidents or exposure was overexertion, accounting for 31.5 percent of cases. The mismatch between the physical demands in the work-

place and the physical capabilities of workers results not only in excessive workers' compensation costs but also in losses from decreased productivity, reduced work quality, increased turnover and diminished worker satisfaction. Also, while there is no specific standard, OSHA does cite under the General Duty Clause, 5(a)(1).

There are many examples of success stories. The OSHA Web site contains over 40 examples of successful ergonomics programs from a wide variety of employers. In some of these case studies, several different exposures where ergonomic risk was found and reduced are detailed.

continued on page 2 ... see Ergonomics: Micro to Macro

Sewage Contamination Evaluation

Sewage contamination can arise from pipe leaks or breaks, drain or toilet backups, and even flood waters. Sewage is often referred to as "black water," which is grossly unsanitary and contains pathogenic agents such as bacteria and viruses, body fluids, feces,

and possibly blood and other contaminants. As such, it is critical that no one comes in contact with sewage contamination unless he or she is fully trained and protected. Do not allow personnel to walk through the affected area as this will spread the contamination and increase the exposure potential.

Secondary contaminants can arise out of black water sources, affecting building materials in the indoor environment if the sewage contamination is not identified and addressed quickly, i.e., within 24 hours. These secondary contaminants include mold and bacterial growth on damaged building materials and endotoxin generation, which arises from the bacterial contamination.

When a sewage incident occurs, in order to evaluate the extent of the areas affected by sewage contamination and the secondary contaminants, an immediate response is critical – through visual observation, moisture content testing and sampling for "markers" of sewage contamination. Development of remediation plans for immediate cleanup are virtually mandatory.

Trained professionals should perform the cleanup activities using appropriate personal protective equipment, cleaners, disinfectants

continued on page 3 ... see Sewage Contamination

THE VISION DAY LETTER

HELPING YOU CLEARLY SET YOUR SIGHTS ON ACHIEVING THE FUTURE YOU REALLY WANT — MAY 2007

Are You Ready for a Big Year?

A Monthly Letter from Debbie and Rob

Debbie Phillips   Rob Berkley

You are receiving this because chances are you've attended Vision Day® -- at least once, maybe twice or even annually. Or, you have been referred to Vision Day by a friend or colleague.

As executive and life coaches, we created Vision Day eight years ago because we needed a strategic plan for our own lives. We were divorced, in a new and exciting relationship with each other, living in separate cities and wanted to create a life together. The world was our canvas but we needed a vision and a plan!

Our coaching clients would need such plans too, we figured. We'd noticed smart professionals set visions and mapped out directions and strategies for their businesses and organizations, but rarely for their own lives and dreams. So, we set up an agenda of fun and challenging exercises and held our own day-long strategic planning session. Vision Day was born.

We picked our theme that first year -- a Year of Adventure. And, a vision: "to help and support people to have lives they dream of." Our personal goals were to combine our lives into a committed partnership; blend our coaching practices into one company, and to create and live an inspiring year and life! (OK, it actually took 13 months to make it all happen ... we hadn't counted on "the

adventure" of Rob popping his Achilles tendon during a tennis match.) If we could set our dreams into motion in a year, you can, too! Since then, hundreds of you have participated in your own Vision Day on Martha's Vineyard or in Naples or both. You have come alone, with your spouse, significant other, business partner or your entire team. Together we've addressed all kinds of goals: to launch businesses; explode your profit in existing ones; plan great years; work through tough transitions; map out books and films; outline fulfilling retirements and endless other combinations.

Daily we hear the results of your successes. Recently Rob wrote a chapter on Vision Day for a book anthology with Stephen Covey called Speaking of Success. In it, he shared Vision Day results and bragged about several of you! Today we launch this monthly newsletter and are extremely proud to feature former software sales executive Laurie Forster who married two of her passions — wine and coaching -- and turned it into a profession! Stay tuned for next month when we unveil details of new program to launch later this year that will make your Vision Day experience even more powerful.

Debbie with The Wine Coach®
Laurie Forster post Vision Day.

Debbie & Rob

CALENDAR

Rob and Debbie's Calendar
May 2007

5/7	Corporate Vision Day Naples
5/9	Rob Corporate Vision Day
5/10	Rob Corporate Vision Day
5/14	Planning Session Las Vegas
5/15	Planning Session Las Vegas
5/16	Mastermind Group Las Vegas
5/17	Mastermind Group Las Vegas
5/20	Rob Corporate Vision Day
5/21	Rob Corporate Vision Day
5/23	NO BS Boston Chapter Meeting (Call Shannon to register (201) 294-5765)
5/23	Debbie Corporate Vision Day NYC
5/24	NO BS Boston Mastermind Meeting (Full)
5/24	Women On Fire Tea Party NYC (Sold Out)
5/26	Partners Vision Day MV

Remaining Summer Vision Day Dates
6/18, 6/29, 7/6, 8/13. Please contact Blue at blue@groupmv.com or 508-696-4949 for an application.

NEWS & NOTES

Well-being expert **Kelley Black** has launched her exclusive *Balancing the Executive Life* program in an exciting new location in New York City. www.balancingtheexecutivelife.com

Maureen Riopelle founder of a foundation and advocate for our nation's 10 million cancer survivors was awarded Cancer Family Care of Cincinnati's Unsung Heroes highest achievement award. www.marymaguirefoundation.org

Victor Cheng of San Francisco delivered on his Vision Day goal to publish his first book "Escaping the Self-Employment Trap." www.morefreedom.com

Allison Barry of Boston, a software sales executive on a well-deserved sabbatical, trekked to New Orleans and volunteered for a week. She reports it was life-changing to participate in the rebuilding of the city.

CELEBRATING **17** YEARS OF WISH GRANTING

MAKE·(A)·WISH

NEWSLETTER

INFORMATION ABOUT WISHES AND THE MAGIC MADE FROM THE MAKE-A-WISH FOUNDATION OF SUSQUEHANNA VALLEY

Special Convoy Issue – 15th Annual Event a Huge Success!

WISH CHILD ON BOARD

On May 9th, we held our 15th Anniversary of the Mother's Day Convoy. This event has become known worldwide as "The Worlds Longest Truck Convoy," with 391 trucks participating this year. I'm sure we will be able to hold the Guinness World Record for many years to come. I contribute this success to everyone involved, including our generous sponsors, the many volunteers who worked hard all day and our committee heads for their excellent planning and organizational skills. The community support, and of course the dedicated truck drivers, many who work all year long to raise money so we can continue to grant the 70 plus wishes this year.

The weather was fantastic and super entertainment, great food, games and a fabulous auction made this year of one of our best years.

Back in 1990, Matt and Heather Strawser (pictured in the top right photo) had a wish to ride in a truck and talk on the CB radio. Who would of thought that 15 years later that wish would turn into "The Worlds Longest Truck Convoy?" With a special presentation, Matt and Heather were riding with the same companies as they did 15 years ago. Heather even had her same driver, Mr. Ron King. Thank you to all who made this possible.

This convoy has been a safe and successful event that has granted many, many wishes over the years, and I hope this will continue far into the future. A very special thanks to everyone!

Randy Etzweiler

Convoy Chairman

see more pictures of our 15th Mother's Day Convoy on page 2

FOR THE PARENTS, CHILDREN, AND STAFF OF VERTYKES LEARNING PLACE

Program Information

Remember to dress your children in play clothes. Painting, sensory play and learning independent feeding skills are all important experiences that can make our clothes messy.

Staff Training News

Do you know that the Department of Public Welfare requires that all staff working in childcare receive a minimum of six hours of training each year? As Hildebrandt Learning Centers continues to provide high quality childcare all staff are required to attend at least 12 hours of annual training. On Saturday, March 29th the staff of VerTykes Learning Place left their homes bright and early for Elizabethtown, PA for the Professional Development Conference entitled *Meaningful Connections That Last*. Staff chose three workshops to attend from the 35 that were offered. You Can't Make Me, Preschool Patter Returns, It Looks Like Fun, But Are They Learning and Games With A Purpose were just a few of the workshops presented. We also enjoyed hearing from two inspirational and informative keynote speakers, Gerry Hart and Leanne Grace. We had 'Show and Share' time where staff from all the Hildebrandt centers displayed items such as documentation boards, lesson plans and special classroom projects. Our staff found the conference a positive experience and they are grateful for this learning opportunity.

You may have noticed the fire truck in front of the center on April 14th and April 23rd. Members of the Berwyn Fire Company were here to provide the VerTykes staff with fire safety training. Evacuation procedures and use of fire extinguishers were a few of the important topics discussed.

Monday April 21 The Segal Puppet Theater brought the Tooth Buddy Tales puppet show to VerTykes Learning Place. This musical and interactive show teaches children about tooth care.

We celebrated the Week of the Young Child April 7 - 11. All the children made handprints that will be put together to make a quilt to remember that we are all devoted to the importance of the early childhood years.

CyberStart Computer

We look forward to the new preschool CyberStart computer that is expected to arrive late this spring. CyberStart is a multi-year technology and education initiative administered by the Pennsylvania Department of Community and Economic Development, in collaboration with the PA Department of Public Welfare. CyberStart embodies a bold vision and a continued commitment by the Commonwealth of Pennsylvania to the use of technology as a means to improve the quality of teaching and expand learning opportunities for young children. Two staff members will receive 12 hours of training and the only cost to us will be the upkeep of the computer after installation.

Healthy Heart Snack Day - Feb 14th!

Illness Policy Reminder: A child's response to fever-reducing medicines is not helpful in determining how sick a child is. Regardless of the presence or height of fever, it is how sick a child looks or acts that is important. The staff working with the child, the director and the parents must work together in deciding whether a child is well enough to attend the center. Hildebrandt Learning Centers has written an illness policy to guide staff and families in keeping our children healthy. If you need a copy or have any questions, please see Stephanie.

Community

United Way
United Way of Chester County

MATTERS

Improving lives by mobilizing communities to create sustained changes in community conditions - 3rd quarter, 2004

United Way Campaign 2004 Kicks Off With Exton Square Partnership

United Way Sets 2004 Campaign Goal of $5 Million Dollars

Here we are, its fall again! The start of school, cooler weather, football season, and yes, the annual United Way of Chester County Campaign. There is a new energy that sparks in the community each fall. What better time for hundreds of corporations and thousands of individuals to unite with a common focus – to support the most critical needs of Chester County.

On Tuesday, September 14, 2004, United Way of Chester County celebrated the launch of the 2004 campaign during a Campaign Kick-Off Event at Exton Square. NBC 10 Meteorologist Amy Freeze gave a "forecast" for the success of the 2004 campaign. The celebration heralded United Way's 2004 campaign goals and commemorated the alliance between United Way of Chester County, Exton Square and Citadel, to build community awareness of United Way. The award winning Downingtown Area School District Band performed during the celebration.

The Lelito Family enjoying each other's company and the 2004 Campaign Kick-Off

Campaign Chair Marci Wright O'Gara, Director of Sales, UPS and Campaign Cabinet Member Andy Hartnett, President, Symmetry Consulting

Through fund raising efforts, including workplace campaigns, corporate contributions, leadership and major giving, and residential donations, United Way is committed to reaching and surpassing its 2004 Campaign Goal of

continued on page 3 ... see Membership Drive

United Way Recognizes Philanthropic Leadership in Chester County

United Way will recognize the generosity of local donors on Saturday, October 16, 2004 at the Chester County Alexis de Tocqueville Society's first annual "Celebrate Philanthropy" event to be held at the Brandywine River Museum in Chadds Ford, Pennsylvania. Local philanthropists will come together to share in an evening of cocktails and light fare. Guests will receive a private tour of the museum's galleries including the Andrew Wyeth and Brandywine Heritage Exhibitions. They will also be treated to a private showing of the special exhibition of Revere's Ride and Longfellow's Legend featuring works by such well known artists as Leonard Everett Fisher, William Robinson Leigh, Charles Santore, Harold Von Schmidt, Lynd Ward, and N.C. Wyeth.

For more information about this event or the Alexis de Tocqueville Society, please contact Claudia Hellebush, President/CPO at United Way of Chester County at 610-429-9400 or Gerald Parsons, President and CEO, CTDI at 610-436-5203.

155

BUSINESS AND PUBLIC AFFAIRS

West Chester University — COLLEGE OF

Providing knowledge, skills, and values consistent with success in a dynamic global community

The Dean's Perspective

The following is an interview with Christopher M. Fiorentino, Ph.D., dean of the College of Business and Public Affairs.

Why is the Association to Advance Collegiate Schools of Business (AACSB) important to West Chester University and the college?

AACSB is the premier accrediting body for business education in the world. Approximately 30 percent of the business programs in the United States currently hold this accreditation. Inclusion in this group is highly prestigious. It certifies that the business program meets the standards set by the profession for high-quality business education. Beyond initial accreditation, programs are expected to strive for continuous improvement in order to maintain accredited status. This ensures that high-quality education remains a focus as we move into the future.

How will it benefit the students, faculty, and University?

The accreditation process focuses on the mission of the program, identifying the goals that will ensure that the mission is central. The students benefit from this process in many ways. A good deal of effort is put into determining the knowledge and skills that students should possess upon graduation from a bachelor's or master's program. To learn how we could better prepare our students for entry-level positions, we have had extensive discussions with business people who hire new college graduates. The faculty benefits from the accreditation because one of the requirements is that sufficient resources be committed to the business program to allow the mission to be accomplished.

Faculty will also benefit from the establishment and maintenance of high standards for students because programs with high standards tend to attract high-quality students. Another major goal of the accreditation process is to ensure that faculty members are highly qualified and current in their disciplines. Well-qualified faculty is the most crucial ingredient in a quality program. The University's reputation will be positively impacted because AACSB accreditation is difficult to obtain and reflects a University-wide commitment to high-quality academic programs. Recognition of this tends to impact positively the overall reputation of the University. This improved reputation also encourages higher levels of financial support for the programs of the University.

What strategic initiatives are planned for the college?

Beyond AACSB accreditation, the next major initiative on the horizon

continued on page 3 ... Dean's Perspective

Clyde J. Galbraith, CPA – 2005 Outstanding Educator Award Winner

Driving Students to Accounting Success
By Nicole Poponi, PICPA Member Relations Coordinator

For more than 30 years, Clyde J. Galbraith, CPA, chair of the Accounting Department, has been dedicated to helping students achieve success in both academics and in their careers. In recognition of his distinguished teaching and involvement in the accounting profession, the PICPA has selected Galbraith as its 2005 Outstanding Accounting Educator. Galbraith is known for his technique of helping students learn auditing skills through a realistic audit practice case. Galbraith acts as a partner in charge of an audit engagement, and students are required to contact him with problems and questions encountered during the simulated audit.

In addition to his primary teaching responsibilities, Galbraith also supervises numerous writing projects and encourages students to enter a variety of writing contests. In 1974, Galbraith began accompanying a group of students to the PICPA's Greater Philadelphia Chapter Annual Student Night and has continued this tradition for the last 31 years. He also attends similar functions of the American Society of Women Accountants (ASWA) and the National Association of Black Accountants (NABA).

Galbraith is the adviser to West Chester University's Accounting Society and the student chapter of NABA, and is the On-Campus

continued on page 3 ... Outstanding Educator

Can Leadership Be Taught?

The answer is yes, according to Evan Leach, associate professor of management at WCU. For the past five years, he has teamed with business leaders from the greater Philadelphia area to teach an innovative leadership course. The course provides students with the latest thinking in leadership research and theory and current business-world applications in order to enhance WCU

continued on page 2 ... Leadership

TICOR TITLE INSURANCE COMPANY

Title Strategies

NEWS AND INFORMATION TO HELP TITLE AGENTS GROW THEIR BUSINESSES AND OPERATE MORE EFFICIENTLY   FALL 2006

Ticor Projects to Double Market Share by Year-end 2007!

Welcome to the premier issue of *Title Strategies*. Ticor Title Insurance Company is pleased to provide this newsletter to our title agents and friends in the hope that the information will help them do more and better business. In this issue, we're pleased to interview Ticor Vice President and Area Manager Jody Jordon.

Jody S. Jordon
Vice President, Area Manager

TS: What markets are you specifically seeking to grow?

JJ: Our goal is to expand our agent base in two of our markets—the Pennsylvania/Delaware market and the New Jersey market.

TS: How will Ticor accomplish such a large goal?

JJ: Ticor is fast becoming the choice of many title agents because of the unparalleled service we provide our agents. In addition, we recognize that far beyond the product, our agents appreciate the many value-added services we bring to the table. Our goal is to help our agents do more business more efficiently.

TS: What are some of the value-added services that you provide to your Ticor agents?

JJ: Ticor works hard to provide benefits and value to our customer base. For example, we run regular seminars and training programs, led by Chuck Travis, Gerry Simon, Sandy Dixon, and other industry leaders. Our agents regularly use these training programs to help keep their staff up to speed on the latest programs and titling strategies. In addition, because of our large support staff and numerous services, Ticor agents can present themselves to their customers as being part of a "national company."

TS: How does the Ticor support staff help its agents?

JJ: Our support staff is superb. We are available to guide our agents through the myriad of challenges that affect them on a day-to-day basis. We provide information and help our agents learn about changes such as the industry trend to adopt Alta forms rather than state-specific forms and how this adoption may affect rates.

TS: Are there any other programs that your offer your agents?

JJ: One of the most popular programs that is available to all Ticor agents is the EC Purchasing program. This program helps our agents reduce some of the operating costs associated with running their businesses. Read more about EC Purchasing in this newsletter.

Ticor Agents Enjoy National Account Pricing on Office Expenses

EC Purchasing is a value-added service that Ticor Title agents can use to reduce the operating costs of their businesses. EC Purchasing combines the purchasing strength of a Fortune 500 company with more than 12,000 individual businesses to negotiate low prices from national vendors of products and services used in the real estate industry. These prices simply are not available to a stand-alone business. Ticor Title agents have access to a broad range of products, including computer equipment, office furniture, copiers, fax machines, office supplies, temporary labor, and low overnight delivery rates from FedEx and UPS. While most Ticor Title agents quickly take part in our FedEx and UPS pricing, an increasing number of agents are also participating in our EC office expense analysis program. Ticor Title agents can receive a free, no-obligation analysis of their expenses by calling 888-387-0223 and speaking with one of the consultants. EC Purchasing consultants usually recommend performing a review of an agent's overnight delivery fees and office supplies. At the agent's discretion, the consultant will continue the analysis on computer equipment, copiers, fax machines, and temporary labor. In all cases, the objective is to provide an apples-to-apples price comparison. It is not uncommon for agents to save 20 percent or more on purchases.

- Office Equipment
- Office Supplies and Services
- Office Furniture
- FedEx and UPS Shipping Services
- Temporary Employment Services

Keep Your Seat Belt Fastened!

The American Automobile Association advises that drivers who are stalled should keep their seat belts in place. If a car breaks down, pull as far off the road to the right as possible. Keep your seat belt on while waiting for help because the car could be hit from behind.

SIGHT FOR LIVING

THE CLEARVISION FOUNDATION NEWSLETTER

INFORMATION TO PROMOTE THE UNDERSTANDING OF VISION PROBLEMS AND TO ASSIST PEOPLE WITH VISION LOSS   2ND QTR – 2005

Vision Insights

In this issue of *Sight For Living*, we're pleased to interview Jean A. Astorino O.D., Low Vision Optometrist and Director of the Sight for Living Vision Center in Media, Pennsylvania.

Dr. Astorino

What brought you to the Sight for Living clinic?
While working at a low-vision facility in western Pennsylvania, I had the opportunity to provide clinical care to patients utilizing a new model of low-vision. It was an eye-opening experience and witnessing the increased success rate of helping the patients by using this model was very exciting. My passion for low-vision care, especially this new methodology, fits the mission of the Clear Vision Foundation and I was pleased to join their team.

What is the old way of practicing low-vision?
Many times magnifiers are sold to patients at a "low-vision store" without the expertise of a doctor and without the proper training. Properly assisting a person with low-vision is more than simply supplying a magnifier. Lighting and contrast enhancement must also be considered to achieve the maximal vision enhancement. A low-vision optometrist or ophthalmologist needs to carefully measure each patient to determine the appropriate combination of magnification device and lighting that will work best with their vision. Not understanding this often results in a person buying a magnifier at a store or from a catalog that ultimately ends up being only half a solution, and most often winds up in a drawer when it fails to function the way he wanted. Proper training is critical to using the devices correctly in order to maximize a person's vision and to getting them over the hurdle of frustration.

What is the new low-vision philosophy?
Doctors and therapists work TOGETHER in a rehabilitation model in order to determine what aids are proper for each patient. The first step in the new method is to measure the patient's vision and determine the power of low-vision aids that is necessary. Next, we evaluate the various low-vision aids in the patient's

continued on back ... see Visual Insights

Successfully Functioning with Low-Vision

For the first time, a full-time, full-service low-vision center is open in Delaware County, Pennsylvania. Sight for Living, a division of the Clear Vision Foundation, is led by Dr. Jean A. Astorino, one of the country's leading low-vision Optometrists. The facility is based on Dr. Astorino's 10-years of field experience including a vision rehabilitation residency at the William Feinbloom Vision Rehabilitation Center, low-vision work at Crozer Chester, Lankenau, and Will's Eye Hospitals in Philadelphia as well as at Pittsburgh Vision Services, a state-of-the-art vision rehabilitation center located in western Pennsylvania.

Individuality is the key to successful low-vision treatments. While some people with macular degeneration may read a newspaper well with a CCTV (a reading machine that uses a video camera to project and magnify reading materials onto a television screen), others may read better with a stand magnifier (featured on back page) because it rests on the page. Others who have low-vision due to diabetes might just need a boost in their reading glasses along with a good reading lamp. Everyone with low vision has the same goal – to see as well as their eyes will let them. While the goal is the same, the road to it has many lanes. The idea is to be patient, examine all the choices, and practice, practice, practice once you find what works well for you. Learn more by calling 610-892-8767.

vision care newsletter

INFORMATION ABOUT OBTAINING CLEAR VISION AND MAINTAINING LONG-TERM VISUAL PRESERVATION   4TH QTR - 2007

Witness to a 20-Year Revolution in Corrective Eye Care

In the last 20 years, I have had the amazing experience of watching a revolution in corrective eye surgery. It seems just like yesterday when we would take a diamond blade and place cuts in the front of the eye, almost its' entire thickness, in a method called, "radial keratotomy," to reshape the front of the eye. This flattened the cornea and obviated the need for glasses in those low myopes. It was difficult to manage astigmatism, a little bit inaccurate, but we had hundreds of very happy patients who did extremely well with this difficult, complex, manual dexterity based procedure.

After the event of laser vision correction, which came into being in 1984 and was adopted in the United States by 1992, I had the pleasure of becoming an FDA-approved investigator at Wills Eye Hospital, where we used the first VISX 2020B laser. At that time, we were limited to correcting one eye in fairly high myopes or people with diopters measuring greater than -10.00. It was really a difficult procedure but still easier than radial keratotomy, and almost immediately it started giving us fantastic results. Once that study was done the technique was introduced in the United States and through out Philadelphia. We got to be among the first in the country to launch the use of the approved VISX laser at Wills Eye Hospital. In 1994, we began treatments with something called "PRK."

Dr. Steven Siepser

> **"We got to be among the first in the country to launch the use of the approved VISX laser ..."**

The next evolutionary step was the presence of early microkeratomes, which allowed us to do LASIK. In 1996 we switched to this procedure, still reserving PRK for people with higher corrections. It has been very interesting to see how this technology progressively advances over time and provides more and more opportunities for significant results in new patients. In this regard, patients often wonder, "Maybe I should wait for something new and better." Actually, what happens with advancing technology is that it increases the scope of our ability to treat more and varied ocular issues.

The laser in the beginning did not treat astigmatism or farsightedness very well. It was excellent with fairly high degrees of nearsightedness where radial keratotomy could not perform. The advent of the newer lasers allowed us to achieve higher and higher corrections, and with LASIK immediate recoveries were noted. The basic technology for these procedures has not changed much since its invention in 1984, and international implementation in 1986. By 1988 much of this had been perfected, but it was years before the FDA allowed this procedure to be performed in the United States.

Newer advances and procedures are always coming forward, and we use those as they are approved in the United States. Initially, we were limited to corrections only

Continued on page 3 ... see 20-Year Revolution

What You Need to Know About Eye Allergies

Allergies are commonly thought to be reactions that make you sneeze, make your eyes watery, or cause nausea and vomiting following ingestion of things you are allergic to. In the worst cases, anaphylactic shock can result. This is the body's reaction to an antigen or something that is foreign; its presence causes a catastrophic reaction in all systems of the body, leading to loss of the ability to breathe and stopping of the heart.

Ocular allergies are usually a different kettle of fish. They are more the humdrum itching and burning of the eyes.

Occasionally more severe symptoms may present as the result of extreme allergies, resulting in extreme swelling and temporary loss of vision. Normal allergies are most commonly caused by dust, pollen, insects and byproducts in the air that are captured in the tear film and precipitate a local reaction in the mucous membranes of the eye, the conjunctiva, setting up recurrent symptoms of watering, burning and the hallmark of allergies, itching. External control involves avoiding dusty environments and being sure the air-handling system has appropriate filtration at home and also at work. By controlling the environment, a great deal of allergic symptoms can be avoided. Animals or dander from animals creates a very common and uncomfortable reaction in certain individuals. The best example is an allergy to cats. In this situation, even being near cats or stroking a cat and then rubbing your eye results in a great many swelling and discomfort as a result of the direct injection of allergens into the eyes. It is best to simply avoid these contact allergens when possible.

The eyelids, being extremely thin skinned, are very commonly the site of an eczematoid reaction or reaction of a more long-term nature, with swelling and reddened appearance of the skin. This sort of reaction is slower to present and more difficult to

Continued on page 2 ... see Eye Allergies

SIANA, BELLWOAR & MCANDREW, LLP
ATTORNEYS AT LAW

BUSINESS ⚖ LAW
REVIEW

BUSINESS LAW • MUNICIPAL DEFENSE • CIVIL LITIGATION • REAL ESTATE • LAND DEVELOPMENT

INSIGHTS AND DEVELOPMENTS IN THE LAW AS IT APPLIES TO YOU AND YOUR BUSINESS OR ORGANIZATION   4TH QUARTER 2006

Special Issue: *Everything You Need to Know About Franchising Your Business*

By Thomas J. Kent Jr.

Existing franchises are expanding at an increasing pace and new franchise concepts are being created in greater numbers than ever before. My law practice is concentrated in the areas of commercial law, franchising, and corporate and partnership matters. With more and more frequency I am asked, "Is my business franchisable?" In this and future issues of Business Law Review, I am going to address many of the questions most often asked about franchising.

What Is Franchising?

First and foremost, franchising is a marketing system, a method for distributing goods and services to the consumer. The most common form of franchising is business format franchising, where a company develops a business system or method for providing products or services, and a trademark identifies all parts of that system or method. Three basic elements determine whether a business is a franchise: use of a trademark or trade name, payment of fees and royalties, and provision of services.

- Trademarks and trade names are the principal assets of franchise companies and are basic to the definition of a franchise.
- Franchisees pay the franchisor a fee for the right to sell a product or service and use its operating system.
- The Federal Trade Commission considers a business to be a franchise if it meets the first two conditions above and it exerts control or provides significant assistance or services.

Business format franchising is the establishment of a chain of businesses operating under a shared trade name or trademark, which pays the franchisor for the right to do business under that name; operates under a specified, controlled business method or format; and/or receives significant assistance or services from the franchisor.

Evaluating Yourself as a Franchisor

As a franchisor, you will provide a wide variety of management services aimed at increasing a franchisee's chances of success. You will be responsible for training new owners, developing new methods and procedures, researching new products or services, providing advice, and sometimes lending franchisees a listening ear. To help you gain insight as to your suitability as a potential franchisor, consider the following questions.

Do you work well with others?

One of the greatest skills you will need to succeed in franchising is the ability to work effectively with other people. Are you team-oriented? Are you willing to listen to the

continued on page 2 ... see Franchising

Should You Be Worried About Your LLC Agreement?

At many law firms, this is not an uncommon story. A client's start-up business becomes successful, and some years later a point of contention arises between the partners. That's when it can get tricky, and expensive.

The problem is that new business partners seldom want to sit down and discuss what might go wrong in their business venture, or how they would split up their assets should one of the partners leave or if the partnership as a whole dissolves. At Siana, Bellwoar & McAndrew, LLP, we believe it is always prudent at the beginning of the relationship to sufficiently plan for one or more of an LLC's partners exiting, and for the total dissolvent of the corporation.

While some LLC agreements include a detailed provision that provides for a partner to buy out another at fair market value, many do not provide for cases where one partner wishes to "fire" another partner. This is not as far-fetched as you may think. For example, one partner may be satisfied with the status quo of the business while another partner wishes to take the business in a new direction. If not planned for in advance or handled ineffectively, a scenario such as this can lead to litigation. Exit provisions must not only explicitly deal with a departing member; they must also deal with a deadlock situation. Here are a few things to consider when forming a new partnership agreement.

1. Make sure that any "exit" provisions require complete separation of the departing member's interest from the LLC.

At the closing of the sale, the purchasing member shall deliver to the selling member a release of all personal liability of the selling member as a guarantor of any indebtedness for borrowed money or other contractual obligation of the company to any person or entity.

continued on page 3 ... see LLC Agreement

SIANA, BELLWOAR & MCANDREW, LLP • 941 POTTSTOWN PIKE, SUITE 200 – CHESTER SPRINGS, PA 19425 • 610-321-5500 • WWW.SIANALAW.COM

The Home Connection

A NEWSLETTER OF FUN FACTS AND USEFUL INFORMATION FOR HOME OWNERS   VOL. 6 ISSUE 13

Hello and Welcome!

This sample issue of *The Home Connection* has been sent to you courtesy of the newsletter professionals at

DYNAMIC COMMUNICATION

Mortgage News

When people refinance their home, they usually seek to replace their current mortgage with a lower-rate mortgage. However, you may also decide to refinance to replace a fixed-rate mortgage loan with an adjustable-rate loan, or vice versa. When you refinance, you can borrow just enough to pay off the mortgage balance you owe, or you can borrow an additional amount in what is called a "cash-out" refinancing.

Funny Bone

Kids Say the Darnedest Things!

The following quote was taken from a grade school teacher's journal used for recording things that students sometimes wrote in papers:

"Syntax is all the money collected at the church from sinners."

To Sell Your House, Add Safety Features and Enhance Curb Appeal

First impressions are a powerful influence on home buyers. They can determine whether buyers fall in love with the idea of your house, and whether they want to look inside or just leave as quickly as possible. It doesn't take much to turn a prospect away. Unkempt grounds are a turnoff. Leaves, unshoveled snow or uncut grass can cost you a sale. Real estate agents suggest walking up to your place to see if there is anything that looks unattractive or out of place.

Sprucing up the front yard is especially important. Planting flowers and shrubs costs some time and money, but can make the difference between a quick sale and one that takes much longer. Always plant flowers that complement the color of your home. Check the trim and repaint it if necessary. Make sure the gutters are clean. Many buyers today are concerned about safety. That's especially true of the one-third of all buyers who are single or single parents. Single women are a fast-growing segment of the market, real estate experts say. Along with the number of bedrooms and the square footage of the house, one single buyer specified an attached garage, a wall around the yard and neighbors. Other safety pluses include

- A security system
- Peepholes in exterior doors
- Lights in the yard and along patios and sidewalks
- A front door and windows that can be seen from the street and not hidden by tall bushes

If you are seeking a home and safety is a priority for you, avoid houses near shopping centers, malls or convenience stores that are open late. Don't buy a home on a busy street, next to a swimming pool or next to an apartment complex that is several stories high, say consultants writing in the Indianapolis Star.

Why You Should Send Your Customers a Newsletter

Next to a personal visit, nothing does more for building business than your own personalized newsletter. A professionally written, designed, and printed newsletter can be one of the most effective marketing weapons you have. Dollar for dollar, newsletters are the most effective marketing tool available. In addition to being a practical and affordable way to keep the vital communication link with your customers, a company newsletter can help grow your business. Here's how they work:

- Newsletters help you retain your customer base, increasing future business
- Stimulated by the reminder, customers are likely to refer friends and neighbors to you
- Most customers will share their newsletter, giving you extra free exposure!
- Stand apart – newsletters will help Differentiate you from your competitors
- Newsletters are an effective way to introduce new products or services

SAVE $99 NOW! Visit www.dynamiccommunication.net and create your on-line newsletter within 14 days of receiving this newsletter, and the $99 set up fee will be waived!!

161

NEWS AND INFORMATION FOR THE CLIENTS AND FRIENDS OF THE GREAT VOICE COMPANY — MONTH YEAR

This is a Variable Box for Your Headline Each Month

A Monthly Letter from Susan Berkley

Lorem ipsum dolor sit amet, consectetuer adipiscing elit, sed diam nonummy nibh euismod tincidunt ut laoreet dolore magna aliquam erat volutpat. Ut wisi enim ad minim veniam, quis nostrud exerci tation ullamcorper suscipit lobortis nisl ut aliquip ex ea commodo consequat. Duis autem vel eum iriure dolor in hendrerit in vulputate velit esse molestie consequat, vel illum dolore eu feugiat nulla facilisis at vero eros et accumsan et iusto odio dignissim qui blandit praesent luptatum zzril delenit augue duis dolore te feugait nulla facilisi. Lorem ipsum dolor sit amet, consectetuer adipiscing elit, sed diam nonummy nibh euismod tincidunt ut laoreet dolore magna aliquam quis

Lorem ipsum dolor sit amet, consectetuer adipiscing elit, sed diam nonummy nibh euismod tincidunt ut laoreet dolore magna aliquam erat volutpat. Ut wisi enim minim veniam, quis nostrud exerci tation ullamcorper suscipit lobortis nisl ut aliquip ex ea commodo

Leslie Wadsworth, voice-over Artist, Seattle, WA

consequat. Duis autem vel eum iriure dolor in hendrerit in vulputate velit esse molestie consequat, vel illum dolore eu feugiat nulla facilisis at vero eros et accumsan et iusto odio dignissim qui blandit praesent luptatum zzril delenit augue duis dolore te feugait nulla facilisi. Lorem ipsum dolor sit amet, consectetuer adipiscing elit, sed diam nonummy nibh euismod tincidunt ut laoreet dolore magna aliquam erat volutpat. Ut wisi enim ad minim veniam, quis nostrud exerci tation ullamcorper suscipit lobortis nisl ut aliquip ex ea commodo consequat.

Duis autem vel eum iriure dolor in hendrerit in vulputate velit esse molestie consequat, vel illum dolore eu feugiat nulla facilisis at vero eros et accumsan et iusto odio dignissim qui blandit praesent luptatum zzril delenit augue duis dolore te feugait nulla facilisi. Lorem ipsum dolor sit amet, consectetuer adipiscing elit, sed diam nonummy nibh euismod tincidunt ut laoreet dolore magna aliquam erat volutpat. Ut wisi enim ad minim veniam, quis nostrud exerci tation ullamcorper suscipit lobortis nisl ut aliquip ex ea commodo.

Vel eum iriure dolor in hendrerit in vulputate velit esse molestie consequat, vel illum dolore eu feugiat nulla facilisis at vero eros et accumsan et iusto odio dignissim qui blandit praesent luptatum zzril delenit augue duis dolore te feugait nulla facilisi. Lorem ipsum dolor sit amet, consectetuer adipiscing elit, sed diam nonummy nibh euismod tincidunt ut laoreet dolore magna aliquam erat volutpat. Ut wisi enim ad minim veniam, quis nostrud exerci tation ullamcorper suscipit lobortis nisl ut aliquip ex ea commodo.

CALENDAR

Rob and Debbie's Calendar June-July 2007

6/7	Rob Corporate Vision Day NYC
6/8	Vision Day Martha's Vineyard
6/15	Vision Day Martha's Vineyard
6/19	Rob No B.S. Chapter Meeting Boston (Call Shannon to register: (201) 294-5765)
6/21-	Rob Corporate Vision Day
22	Philadelphia
6/22	Debbie Women on Fire Tea Party NYC
7/9-	Rob Corporate Vision Day Martha's
10	Vineyard
7/11	Rob No B.S. Chapter Meeting Boston
7/17	Rob Annual Mastermind Retreat on Martha's Vineyard (Full)
7/22	Debbie speaking at National Governors Association, Traverse City, MI

Remaining Summer Vision Day Dates

6/29, 7/13, 8/10, 8/13. Please contact Blue at blue@grbupmv.com or 508-695-4949 for info and an application.

NEWS & NOTES

Well-being expert **Kelley Black** has launched her exclusive *Balancing the Executive Life* program in an exciting new location in New York City. www.balancingexec.com

Maureen Riopelle founder of a foundation and advocate for our nation's 10 million cancer survivors was awarded Cancer Family Care of Cincinnati's Unsung Heroes highest achievement award. www.marymaguirefoundation.org

Victor Cheng of San Francisco delivered on his Vision Day goal to publish his first book "Escaping the Self-Employment Trap" www.morefreedom.com

Allison Barry of Boston, a software sales executive on a well-deserved sabbatical, trekked to New Orleans and volunteered for a week. She reports it was life-changing to participate in the rebuilding of the city.

MONTH YEAR

Hello! We are pleased to send you this monthly issue of *FYI*. It is our way of saying that you are important to us and we truly value your business. Please feel free to pass this newsletter on to friends and neighbors. Enjoy!

. . . .

A MONTHLY NEWSLETTER TO INFORM AND ENTERTAIN OUR CUSTOMERS

Business Writing Lesson on Active and Passive Voice

Do you understand the difference between active and passive voice? If not, don't panic. Most people would have trouble defining them or coming up with good examples. But Stephen King, the yarn-spinner of horror who has been giving us the creeps for years, explains it clearly in his book *On Writing*. Verbs, he says, come in two types – active and passive. "With an active verb, the subject of the sentence is doing something. With a passive verb, something is being done to the subject of the sentence." King suggests avoiding the passive voice whenever possible. King says he believes that some writers are drawn to the passive voice because they believe it lends their writing some type of authority or even majesty – and that makes them feel safe.

Here are some of King's examples:

Passive: The meeting will be held at seven o'clock.
Active: The meeting's at seven.

Passive: My first kiss will always be recalled by me as how my romance with Shayna was begun.
Active: My romance with Shayna began with our first kiss. I will never forget it.

Passive: The rope was thrown by the writer.
Active: The writer threw the rope.

The World Is Rich with Opportunity

Do you think that opportunity only knocks once? If you do, Richard Carlson, author of *Don't Worry, Make Money*, says you're buying into one of the most perpetuated myths in our culture. Carlson argues that this kind of thinking inspires people to do things they really do not want to do, based on a "never enough to go around" mind-set that just isn't true. Thinking that it's now or never often encourages bad decision making. For instance, he explains, you might take a job you do not want or move to an area that doesn't

really sit well with you. The world we live in is rich with ever-increasing opportunities, he says. The world is in need of creative people, and everyone has his or her own gifts and talents to offer. You just have to figure out how it's open to work for you. There are thousands of jobs out there that you can do. There are thousands of business opportunities. But, Carlson says, first you have to overcome your fear: the fear of not having enough. The fear that you only get one shot and then it's over. It's a big lie. Your life will be filled with great opportunities over and over again.

Monthly Joke

Things you'll never hear Dear Old Dad say

• Darn it … I'm lost. Can you believe that? I'll just stop here and ask directions.

• Sweetie, now that you've turned 13, I think you should be allowed to do whatever you want.

• I really like the attitudes of your friends. They seem angry and disrespectful, and I see the value in that.

• I just want you to have my credit card and new car so that you can have a great time. No curfew. Go ahead, go wild!

• While your mother and I are away for the weekend, I thought you might want to have a party. Here's the key to the liquor cabinet.

• I think a tattoo of the devil would look great on you. Let's go down to the parlor—I'm paying.

• You don't need to work for your spending money. Shoot, I make enough. How much do you need?

– Adapted from Ahajokes.com

. . . .

Monthly Quote

On action: *I like things to happen; and if they don't happen, I like to make them happen.*

– *Winston Churchill*

Bonus Resource #1

The Newsletter Guru's Bonus Resource # 2
The Newsletter Guru Answers Your Questions!

On my No Hassle Newsletter "Interview the Experts" monthly coaching call for December 2008, I spent much of the time answering several subscribers' questions. Many of these questions and answers have been worked into the book's chapters. Here is some other great stuff that I didn't quite squeeze in. Since the following pages are a transcript of the rest of that call, please be aware that it is unedited.

Hello everyone. This is Jim Palmer, the Newsletter Guru. I'd like to welcome you to this call, our No Hassle Newsletters call for December. I'd like to especially welcome all of our new subscribers this month. I believe we have a record number of new subscribers. I think we've actually quadrupled our membership in the last two months, which is pretty exciting. We now have subscribers, in addition to the United States and many, many of the states, we've Australia, England, The Netherlands, Mexico, Canada; so again, a big welcome to everyone that's on the call.

As I mentioned on a number of occasions, I'm doing something a little different this month. The entire call is going to be dedicated to kind of answering your questions that you've had, and that I've received over the last several months. I've been collecting the questions, putting them in a folder. Since I announced this call a few weeks ago people have e-mailed me a number of questions.

Because we have so many subscribers that are in different time zones in the United States and different countries, some people are actually sleeping right now, or should be I guess. They always e-mail their questions in and then they get to listen to either a replay of the call, or they get to listen to the CD.

Right now we're currently working on the February edition of Success Advantage and, man, that sounds strange to be working on February and it's December. But as you know, we're always working 30 days in advance. It's just my way of helping to keep you on track, and keep you on schedule with your newsletter. So in early January you're going to get everything you need to mail out your February issue in plenty of time.

We'll be getting the February edition, you'll be getting that in print and via the Web site right around the first of the month. We might be, you know the second or third because of the holidays and people taking some time off.

The new two-page color newsletter, FYI, that we started including with the January issue last month is getting rave reviews. People are loving that. I've gotten a lot of really nice comments that people are liking that I actually kept in the header. It's fully designed. You don't need to kind of create your own header and drop it in that way. So people are really liking that.

The content, as I provide it, is really skewed towards B2B. But again, since it's sent to you in Word, you can obviously edit that and kind of put in the articles that you want. With all of the newsletter templates that we provide you're free to edit and print these newsletters as you wish and send them out to your subscribers, your customers, your clients, your prospects, whatever you choose.

Let me tell you a little bit about what we're working on for next year. Right now, we're currently working on a really awesome strategy that's just going to add just unbelievable value to this whole program. We are looking at a way where we're going to be able to provide custom headers and some special articles written for several different niche industries. For instance if you're a realtor, mortgage broker, perhaps you're a trial attorney, there's a number of different specialties within the attorney field, there's coaches and things like that.

We are currently negotiating with some very talented writers, trying to find just the right mix of folks that can provide us with some articles on a regular basis. The exciting thing about this is that as you get the Success Advantage newsletter each month and it's filled with 24 pages of really good, what I call customer-loving articles, then what you need to do is put in a couple articles specific for your industry. What we're aiming to do is even fill that gap, that done-for-you newsletter gap even closer. Because what I like to tell people is that each month when you get Success Advantage, you're about 80-90% complete with your newsletter. I'm hoping to even close that gap even more.

What we're doing, in addition to the articles is I'll custom create a bunch of different header graphics that would fit right at the top of the newsletter that you'll be able to just pop in there. That's about all I can tell you about that right now. It's going to be very, very exciting. I'm hoping to have that done, most likely in early February. I might be announcing it in January. Keep cracking the whip here, but people do like to take some time off here around the holidays. You're going to love it; that's all I can tell you. So just stay tuned for that.

As I mentioned last month, we are now offering a Master Reseller version of No Hassle Newsletters. Now if you are someone that is looking to provide done-for-you newsletters to your herd, in other words a number of people have approached me that are either coaches or they're kind of gurus in their own field, whether it be, you know in the automotive repair industry or things like that; and some of the services that you provide to your customers, you'd like them to have a newsletter. If you're a regular subscriber to No Hassle Newsletters, the content that I give you with Success Advantage newsletter and the templates, the newsletter templates that I provide are for your use and your business, for you to send out to your customers and clients and prospects. If you'd like to use those newsletter templates, or take my content, repackage it and resell it as a service from you to your customers, the way to do that is to sign up for one of our Master Reseller licenses. That's the only way that you legally have the right to use, resell and in any other way kind of profit from distributing the content and the newsletter templates that I'm providing your business. It's really very easy to do that. Just go to SuccessAdvantage.net, scroll down to where I have the pricing and you'll see. You'll see the pricing for the Master Reseller version.

I am really, really excited to announce something that I've been talking about for the last couple weeks. In fact since I got back in early November from the Glaser-Kennedy info-summit, I am now ready to say that my Concierge Print and Mail in Demand Service is now live. It actually went live, literally about 35 minutes ago. So that's pretty exciting.

Let me tell you a little bit about that. I have teamed up with my friend and my business partner Bobby DeRocko to create really just what we feel is an amazingly simple program. One of the things that people were talking to me about is, well, Jim, we love the newsletters, the content, but really, how do I get the thing printed and mailed?

What we did is we created a program where we make it just incredibly quick and easy for you to get your monthly newsletter out the door and into your customer's hands. Let me tell you a little bit about Bobby Deraco. We've been business partners for about five years now. Bobby owns one of the largest print management companies in the country. Together with what Bobby does with his clients and the volume that I bring through my corporate business and No-Hassle Newsletters, Success Advantage and some other things, we together have about $14 million worth of print-buying power that we bring to the table.

What we've done is we've set up a program where even small orders qualify for big savings, okay? When you go to TheNewsletterGuru.com under products and solutions, you'll see a link for the Newsletter Guru's Concierge and Print and Mail On-Demand Service. That'll take you to a page where you're going to see three different price charts, okay?

At the Web site you're going to see three price charts for the three types of newsletters that we provide with No Hassle Newsletters. There's a two-page black-and-white, there's four-page black-and-white, there's two-page color, which is for the FYI newsletter.

Now the great thing about this is because of the volume that I do personally with Bobby, and again Bobby's collective buying power, we've set up pricing so that even if you're ordering, you know, 100, 200, 300 newsletters, you're going to get some really, really great pricing. Pricing's actually as low as $0.69 each for a two page newsletter. And that's printing, that's processing your mailing list, and that's even including postage.

The way the system works, is again very simple. You're just going to click on the order now link, which is right below the price chart. If you're doing a two-page black-and-white, you're going to click order now and you're going to basically type in the quantity that you want to print and mail. You'll just follow through as if you're ordering anything on line and pay for it. Immediately upon paying for the print newsletter, you're going to be taken to a link where you're going to get a special e-mail. That's going to be your opportunity to send your mailing list and your newsletter directly to Bobby and his staff. We've made it very, very simple. Again, it's called the Newsletter Guru's Concierge Print and Mail

On-Demand Service. Check that out at TheNewsletterGuru.com.

As I've mentioned, we do have several new subscribers this month. I think there's about 35 or 40 folks who are new to the program, again, a big welcome to you. I want to let you know if you're in this call for the first time I do mute all the lines ahead of time so we can get a nice clean recording. I will un-mute the lines in a few moments when we start doing the Q&A portion.

I've been on so many calls as a guest and some folks don't mute their calls and you hear a lot of background noise, dinner plates chattering and a lot of different noise. I choose to mute the calls upfront and then we'll open up the phones shortly.

As always, there's three ways that you can ask a question during the Q&A portion of the call; which in this month is going to be most of the call. If you're listening via the web link, which is the link that you get in the e-mail, you can type your question right into the Q&A window. I do see that. I'm sitting in front of my monitor right now. You can also e-mail me at

<u>Jim@TheNewsletterGuru.com</u>, and of course, you can ask your question live.

Again, since some folks are in different time zones, different countries, I've already been e-mailed a number of different questions. We'll get those answered here pretty quick.

For next month's coaching call, which will be in January, I am scheduling to have Bobby DeRocko as my special guest. In addition to printing most of my newsletters for the last five years and a lot of other print jobs for me, Bobby has a great deal of talent. He's got a lot of ideas on customer-relationship marketing. He's also going to share some tips with you on kind of print design, and how to save money working with your various print projects that you may have in your company. If you're doing brochures or what have you, you're going to learn something on this call. The call is Wednesday, January 21st and of course I'll be sending out my usual series of e-mail reminders.

Let me see, that's all we have for housekeeping. So we're going to get ready to go with tonight's call. Before we get to the questions, I want to kind of share with you 10 strategies that have significantly helped me grow in the last couple years. I am a huge reader. I read a lot of different things, *Think and Grow Rich, Psychocybernetics.* One of my favorite authors is my friend Lee Milteer. I've heard some of the strategies that I'm going to talk about in many different books. Lee actually puts out a very good e-zine. I recently saw these in her e-zine. I'm going to share these with you. Here we are, typically at the end of the year we're taking we're kind of taking stock of where we've been and what we've accomplished this year. And we're also looking forward to the next year, 2009. I just want to help everybody to do exceptionally well in 2009, no matter what's happening around us. Because we know there's a lot of negativity going on. (This information has been worked into Chapter Nine.)

What you want to do, by the way, when I give you the Success Advantage, and I give you, as you know a four-page newsletter template. I pre-populate the four-page newsletter template with a number of articles and there's also space for you to fill in some of your own articles. What you want to do there is just write your article in Word and just copy and paste it into a text box in the newsletter.

At the very top you have your picture box where it says this is where your header goes. If I'm not mistaken I think that's eight inches by one and a half inches, something like that. What you want to do is design your header. If you don't have access to a graphic designer or you're not for instance good at publisher or something like that, you can easily just create in Word, using Word, or you can create a name for your newsletter and just save it. You do have to save it to either a JPEG or print it to a PDF. Then you can insert that PDF up into that picture box up at the top.

The one thing I'll tell you is, and this is where some people may get stuck a little bit, is you have to insert it as the right size. When you setup your page make

177

sure you set it up to be the exact size that I'm telling you. Once you put in your header, you put in your own article. For instance on page one you may put your work stuff article, on the back of page four is where you're going to put your personal monthly message. This is a place for you to kind of show your personality, where you want to have people learn something about you. If you're a brick and mortar business, or if you're an Internet-based business where you don't have face-to-face meetings like an accountant would, this is where you want to open up a little bit and kind of make a personal, kind of people-to-people connection.

Our next question is one that I sometimes get from new subscribers. As I mentioned we have quite a few on this call, so let me address it. I actually go this question, Jim, I am a new Success Advantage subscriber, now what do I do? So I actually kind of covered that a little bit, but again, each month you're going to get the Success Advantage newsletter, which is the content. That's my newsletter to you. You get that as a Word document. You also get that in the mail; I provide that in the mail for - the main reason I do that is people like to read that and circle it. A number of my clients have assistants that actually put out their newsletter. What they'll do is go through the Success Advantage newsletter and they'll circle articles or put a check mark around them and give them to their assistant. That way they know which articles they want to go into the four-page template.

I do provide the four-page newsletter template as four separate pages. So when you download it from the Web site it's, for instance January newsletter page one, page two, et cetera. I do that for two reasons. Number one, it helps to prevent re-flow. So if try to put in a very large article, for instance, in the space on page one, it keeps it from flowing all into the other pages, so you're kind of forced to work with one page.

The reason I present it as four separate pages is so that if you want to do a two-page newsletter you can simply use page one and page four and just basically you have an 8-1/2x11, two page newsletter printed front and back, so you can do that. If you want to have a six page, you can obviously use page two and page three and just do copies and just put in some different articles on those pages.

Essentially you just open it up in Word, and because you're in Word, you have Text boxes and you have picture boxes. If you want to remove an article you just run your cursor over it, you highlight it and hit backspace or delete. That article goes out. Then you copy and paste either another article from Success Advantage or one that you write yourself into the template. Once you save it, you are then free to, you can print it out on your home printer. You can send it to Kinko's, or Office Max or Staples. Or you can use our new Concierge Print and Mail On-Demand Service.

That's kind of what you do. The other things that you get with No Hassle Newsletters is I give you an e-zine template. I give you instructions on how to edit that using what's called WYSIWYG, which stands for What You See Is What You Get software. It's free. When you download this free software and open up your e-zine template, it'll basically look very similar to a Word document. You can kind of change out an article. You can copy and paste your own kind of personal monthly message into the top. You can insert a header or simply type out the name of your name of your e-zine. You save it and then you can insert that into Outlook or Outlook Express and send it that way.

I will tell you that I provide that e-zine template because a lot of subscribers that I have are kind of new to business and they're starting out. They have lists of 100 to 200 customers. I think that's okay to send an e-zine using Outlook or Outlook Express. What I suggest, however, is that you break down your list into kind of manageable chunks, maybe 25 to 50 people at a time.

What you want to do is you address it to yourself and then you blind carbon-copy, which is the BCC function. You put all your addresses in the blind carbon-copy section so everybody that gets your newsletters are not seeing everybody else's e-mail, just a good way to protect your list that way.

If you get over 150 to 200 names and you're doing it on a regular basis and you're feeling it's a little cumbersome to do it multiple times, that's when you need to get into either a list service or another professional e-zine type company like Constant Contact is very good. If you start sending huge volumes like that, you have the potential for getting tagged as a spammer; just want to give you that warning.

So I hope that answers that question, again it's pretty simple. A related question that I get is how many times can we use the templates? That's a very good question. I kind of covered that in the beginning but I'll go over that again. As a subscriber, as a regular subscriber to No Hassle Newsletters you can take those templates and use them as many times as you want promoting your business.

For instance, I have one client that has, he owns three different businesses, He gets that four page template and he actually just drops in three or four different

182

headers and he writes a different personal monthly message to each customer base but the rest of the newsletter's the same. Here he is, paying basically the $47 a month for the silver program and he gets the four page newsletter. He did have somebody create a nice masthead for each one. Again he drops in the masthead. In each version he writes a personal monthly message for each business and the rest of the newsletter is the generic "the other stuff". And he now has three different newsletters that he can send out to his three different businesses.

You are free to use, as a subscriber, these newsletters, as much of the content as you want. And any newsletter, or if you're sending out your own e-zine you can use any of the articles that I'm giving you in Success Advantage in promoting your business to your clients and your prospects.

Just to recap, if you're using, if you like to use the newsletter, kind of turn it around, offer it as your own to your own customer base, you need to have a Master Reseller license. That's the only way to legally do that. You can get into a lot of trouble if you're reselling it, making money on my products that should really only have a license to promote your own business.

Anybody have a question? Next question's how often do you recommend sending an e-zine? Well what I like to say is that you certainly want to do your monthly printed newsletter monthly; hence the monthly printed newsletter. So you definitely want to be sending it out monthly. By the way, let me also mention I strongly, strongly, strongly encourage you to send your monthly printed newsletter at the same time each month. That's one of the reasons I give you everything you need 30 days in advance.

By the time you get No Hassle Newsletters, you get your templates, you've got a month to get your own article written and get it dropped in; you can actually be ready for instance, let's say you get the January issue and January 2nd, by February 1st you can be launching your February newsletter. Again we just keep the cycle every 30 days.

I have some additional questions about newsletter marketing in general that I want to answer. The question is, is it wise to send the same newsletter to different customer groups? I own a business that has both retail and wholesale customers. Well sometimes, but likely not. More than likely, it's not a good idea, and I'll tell you why, but have no fear, it's not as difficult as you think.

Number one, for this specific subscriber who has both retail and wholesale customers, obviously you're going to write a separate personal monthly message because if you're talking with wholesale customers you're generally talking about even a different language. Wholesalers have different language than retailers. You want to, there's going to be certain jargon or buzzwords you might use. Your monthly special offer, obviously needs to be tailored two different ways.

And of course, if you're going to do a customer spotlight, which I like to do, I think it's a good idea to always kind of spotlight one of your customers, obviously you're going to spotlight one of your wholesale customers in a different newsletter. You're going to spotlight one of your retail customers because if you do anything else, if you do create one newsletter, you're going to just generate some confusion. People are going to be a little confused about what you're doing.

Let me give you a tip on how you can make this a little bit easier on yourself. The basic shell of the newsletter, and let's talk about the FYI, which is the two-page color newsletter that I give you every month as a subscriber. The two places that you can customize that - you can customize the whole thing, but the only place you really have to customize is put an article on the front, which is your work stuff; put in your contact information which is probably the same I'm guessing. And on the back page you're going to put your personal monthly message.

So what you do is you write an article that's geared toward your wholesale clients. And you write an article that's geared towards your retail clients. You open up the

FYI newsletter in Word. You drop in your retail newsletter. And then you save as, and simply call it FYI wholesale, and then you drop in the wholesale newsletter article on the front and save that.

You open up page two; fill in your contact information, drop in your personal monthly message to your retailers and save that. And then do a save as and call it FYI commercial, or wholesale, and then you drop in that message. Now it really didn't take you that much time. The rest of the newsletter's fine. The humor, the other kind of interesting articles and tidbits, what I call the other stuff, that is usually good for both wholesale, retail, B2B, B2C, there's really not a huge amount of difference there. The short answer again is, yes, you've got to use two newsletters. But I've just shown you how easy it can be.

Now we're getting close to the hour here. So let me talk a little bit about my Concierge Print and Mail On-Demand service. What I've done, is if you go to that Web site, again, you go to TheNewsletterGuru.com. You'll see a link for the Newsletter Guru's Concierge Print and Mail On-Demand Service. The three steps on ordering, is you're going to see three price charts. The two-page black and white, four-page black and white, and two-page color.

You will see about eight different categories and it's 100-199, 200-299, 300-399, all the way up until 800 and above. Now what you're going to notice on all three price charts is that the 100-199, the per piece is quite a bit higher than the rest of them, okay? And the reason for that is the minimum quantity to mail a newsletter using standard mail is 200 pieces. That's just a post office regulation. So if you're going to mail between 100 and 199, we have to mail those using first-class postage. So that costs a little bit more.

So what you do, let's say your mailing list is 200, you're going to do 200 two-page black and white newsletters, Those we will print. We will process your mailing lists. We'll apply postage. We'll deliver them to the post office for $1.27 each, postage included. I have checked this any number of ways. I actually have some subscribers who've been asking me about this service. A couple of them have sent me quotes for local printers and we are a good 15-20% less than most of the places you're going to find locally.

Again, Bobby has given us the volume pricing based on the total volume that I am doing with all my companies with his business. He knows, I'm his customer, in addition to his partner. He wants to keep me happy. So he knows these are some small orders. There's going to be a lot of small orders. But it's a good way for us to offer kind of a value-added service. I don't have a big mark-up on this. You're my client. You're my No Hassle Newsletter subscriber. This is just a way for me to give you another way to, again, I'm always looking for ways to bridge the gap providing a done-for-you service.

What you would do is click order now. You go to the next window and you're going to add in the quantity of the newsletters that you want printed and mailed. Let's say that you have 200 newsletters and your mailing list, which is an Excel spreadsheet.

I actually show you a sample of what that looks like. It's very, very simple. Essentially kind of going across the top with column A, B, C. you've got first name, last name, street address, city, state and zip, very, very simple.

You cannot set up a mailing list wherein box A you have everything. You don't have John Smith, 123 Main Street, Springfield, IL, 20016. Each one of those has to be in a separate box. Again, I show you a picture of exactly what that looks like.

You order, you put in 200 newsletters in the quantity ordered window and you just push recalculate and you get to the payment window. You pay for your order with a credit card. At the payment window, you're going to see two options. I give you an option to see a PDF proof of your newsletter. Now most of the folks are basically using my designs and they're putting in their articles and pictures. When they go to print it, they print and create a PDF. So what you're going to send us is a PDF of your newsletter, and you're going to send us your mailing list.

Essentially we will print whatever your PDF looks like. If, however, you want to see the newsletter, again for a little piece of mind, or maybe you're not sure it's going to look right, we can do that. There is a $20 fee for that. The reason is we have to get what's called a Pre-Press Person to generate the PDF of your newsletter and then e-mail it to you, wait for you to e-mail it back with your okay and then we move forward. So $20 actually doesn't even begin to cover our cost there with the labor, but we're just going to keep it very, very reasonable.

The other option you have is if you want to order some extra newsletters to hand out on appointments, on sales calls, maybe put them on your front counter in the office, or if you're a brick and mortar store you can put them up at the front counter or whatever, you can order quantities of 50 or more, anything over 50; 50, 51, 52, 150, whatever you want just increase your quantity. What we do, it is the same price. So in terms of 200 it's $1.27. The amount that's built into that price for postage is what we use to box your newsletters and to pay for the UPS charge to your house. So that's why it's the same price.

If you want to get a PDF proof, you just click that button. If you want to order printed copies to receive via UPS, you order your printed copies. You pay for your order. You're immediately taken to a page and it says, great, we're ready to proceed. We're ready to receive your newsletter. You click a link that's a special link that's going to go to Bobby and his team. I'm going to see a copy of it. It tells you to attach your PDF newsletter. It tells you to attach your Excel file mailing list. You hit send and you are done.

The whole process, we've run it, I've been testing this thing for 10 days. I've had other people test it. You can get in and pay for your order, send it to us in about five minutes or less. And then you're done. Now you don't have to get it done yourself. You don't have to print labels. You don't have to get your daughter, or your niece, or your neighbor to fix labels and stamps. You get your Success Advantage. You create your newsletter and you sign up, send it to us. And you're done and you're out the door.

We are out of time. I want to thank you very much for being part of this telecast. You'll be receiving a CD of the call in a few weeks with the February newsletter. Our next call is Wednesday, January 21st. I'll be sending you the normal e-mail reminders about the call. Again next month I'm planning to have Bobby Deraco from Synapse Print Management as my special guest.

I want to wish everyone a very safe and happy holiday. And remember, folks, great newsletters are sales letters in disguise. So go out and sell something. So until next time, this is Jim Palmer, the newsletter guru. I look forward to sharing this time again with you next week. Good night everybody.

Made in the USA
Middletown, DE
31 May 2022

66437411R00119